AUTHOR'S NOTE

Route 66 has been part of our family story for a long time. Keith and his father were born and raised in St. Louis and spent years driving stretches of the Mother Road together. Jake's great-grandfather owned a farm right on Route 66. In more recent years, Keith has regularly traveled portions of the road between Tulsa Oklahoma and Chicago Illinois for family medical trips, and Jake's young son discovered the road in his own way through a love for the disney movie *Cars*.

Those family connections helped spark this book. Over the years, we read a number of Route 66 books, and while many were informative, some felt a little distant from the warmth, humor, and personality that make this road unforgettable. We wanted to create the Route 66 book we wished existed, one that felt lively, approachable, and fun while still honoring the history that makes the Mother Road so meaningful.

With Route 66 reaching its one hundredth anniversary in 2026, the moment felt right. This road is more than pavement. It is memory, movement, hardship, hospitality, neon, curiosity, and story. It belongs to the people who built it, preserved it, traveled it, and kept believing it was worth remembering.

We hope this book makes you smile, teaches you something new, and inspires you to take a closer look at the places, people, and legends that have kept Route 66 alive for a century.

Jake & Keith Provance

ABOUT THE AUTHORS

Jake Provance is an Oklahoma writer, publisher, and co-author who enjoys creating books that feel personal, accessible, and rooted in real life.

Keith Provance is a veteran author and publishing professional who has spent decades helping bring books into the world.

Together, Jake and Keith bring a father-and-son perspective to the Mother Road, blending family story, historic curiosity, and a deep appreciation for the communities that continue to keep Route 66 alive.

CELEBRATING 100 YEARS OF ROUTE 66 • 1926-2026
ROUTE
66
OFFICIAL CENTENNIAL EDITION
100 YEARS
CENTENNIAL EDITION
100 YEARS OF LEGENDS,
DINERS & ROADSIDE WONDERS
BUCKLE UP.
Crazy facts, wild stories, fun trivia, quick history,
and must-see stops—served hot.
JAKE AND KEITH PROVANCE

Route 66 Centennial Edition
100 Years of Legends, Diners & Roadside Wonders
Copyright © 2026 by Jake and Keith Provance
ISBN: 978-1-7344605-8-2

Published by Life Impact Publishing
P.O. Box 701403
Tulsa, Oklahoma 74170

ACKNOWLEDGMENTS

We are deeply grateful to the people who showed interest in this book, shared their time and insight, and continue to serve the Route 66 community with such care.

A special thank you to

Rhys Martin, President, Oklahoma Route 66 Association

Julie Akers, Executive Director,
Oklahoma Route 66 Association

Beth Murray, President, California Historic
Route 66 Association

Kelli Shapiro, PhD, Public historian and
historic preservationist

Miranda Meixner, Historic Route 66 Association of Arizona

Nikki, Historic Route 66 Association of Arizona

Thank you for your contributions to this book, and even more, for the work you do to preserve, celebrate, and strengthen the Route 66 community. The Mother Road endures because people like you keep its stories alive.

INTRODUCTION

Roll down the window and listen for a second.

Hear it? It's the low hum of tires on old pavement, the clink of a diner coffee cup, the crackle of a neon sign warming up for the night. For a hundred years now, that sound has meant one thing to travelers: Route 66.

When this skinny line of asphalt first wound its way from Chicago to Santa Monica in 1926, it wasn't meant to be a legend. It was just a practical idea—tie a patchwork of local roads into one continuous route and suddenly the country feels smaller, more reachable. Truckers used it. Dust Bowl families followed it. Soldiers shipped off for war along it. Hollywood stars and rock 'n' rollers cruised it. Over time, the "Main Street of America" picked up a second name: the "Mother Road," because everything seemed to run to her and from her.

But this book is not here to give you a lecture on highway policy or make you memorize dates.

Route 66 has survived this long because of stories, not statistics. It's the giant concrete whales and muffler men waving over the rooftops. It's the motel that somehow still glows the same shade of neon blue it did in your grandparents' childhood. It's the waitress who's been topping off travelers' coffee for forty years and knows every kind of road-trip heartbreak and honeymoon by heart.

That's the Route 66 we're here to celebrate. So instead of conquering Route 66. Let it happen to you. Pull over when something makes you curious. Talk to the diner owner. Read the plaque even if it's sun-faded and slightly dramatic. Take the photo you'll swear you didn't need. Because somewhere between the roadside oddities and the quiet stretches of pavement, the Mother Road does what she's always done—she turns regular miles into stories worth keeping.

So go on. Start where you are, head the direction that feels right, and if you miss a stop... congratulations. You just gave yourself a reason to come back.

THE HISTORY

Cars were rattling along dirt tracks and wagon roads that vanished in the rain. Towns begged to be connected. Farmers wanted better ways to ship crops. Soldiers coming home from World War I had seen paved roads in Europe and wondered why their own country still relied on mud. Out of that restlessness came a big idea: stitch together a true national highway system.

Drawing a Line Across a Continent

In the 1920s, businessmen and visionaries started sketching routes on maps. One of the loudest voices was an Oklahoma entrepreneur named Cyrus Avery. He pushed hard for a diagonal road that would slice through the middle of the country—from the Great Lakes to the Pacific—linking farm towns, oil fields, and up-and-coming cities like Tulsa and Oklahoma City.

In 1926, the government made it official. U.S. Highway 66 was designated as one of the original U.S. numbered highways, running about 2,448 miles from Chicago, Illinois, to Santa Monica, California, across eight states. Road signs began going up the next year.

Avery didn't just want a road; he wanted a brand. He leaned into the nickname "Main Street of America," promising that this wasn't some lonely bypass—it was the road that ran right past your front door, through the hearts of small towns and big dreams.

Before long, the nicknames piled up. In Oklahoma it was promoted as the Will Rogers Highway, honoring the state's beloved humorist. Later, thanks to a novelist with a sharp eye for human struggle, it would pick up its most famous title of all: the Mother Road.

Dust, Desperation, and the "Mother Road"

The 1930s didn't treat the heartland kindly. When the Great Depression collided with the Dust Bowl, farm families across Oklahoma, Texas, Arkansas, and Kansas watched their fields turn into cracked earth and flying grit. For many, the only option was to load what they could onto a truck and head west, hoping California would live up to the rumors.

They poured onto Route 66.

John Steinbeck followed them in his 1939 novel *The Grapes of Wrath*, devoting a chapter to this new highway and calling it "the mother road, the road of flight." The Joad family in the book was fictional, but their story mirrored thousands of real journeys: overloaded cars, kids perched on mattresses, hand-painted signs on the back bumper that might as well have read, *Last Chance*.

Route 66 in those years was not romantic. It was hot, crowded, dusty, and tough. But it was also possibility poured into concrete and gravel—a path out, a promise that life might be better somewhere over the next hill.

War, Work, and the Great American Road Trip

Then came World War II. Once again, 66 proved itself useful. The road channeled troops, military convoys, and materials to bases and factories across the Southwest. Small towns saw new money, new faces, and new reasons to stay open late.

When the war ended, a new America hit the pavement. Gas was cheap, car ownership exploded, and suddenly the country had both the wheels and the paychecks to go exploring. Families piled into big chrome-lined machines with tailfins and bench seats, kids fighting over the window while Dad watched the temperature gauge on long desert grades.

On Route 66, business boomed. Mom-and-pop motels strung colored bulbs along their eaves. Diners advertised "Chicken Fried Steak" and "Air Conditioning" with equal pride. Trading posts promised real Native American jewelry (sometimes more "real" than others). Neon signs didn't just tell you where to turn—they shouted, winked, and buzzed against the night.

Hollywood noticed. So did musicians. A snappy tune called "(Get Your Kicks on) Route 66" hit the airwaves in 1946 and never really left, getting covered by everyone from Nat King Cole to the Rolling Stones. TV followed in the 1960s with a series simply titled *Route 66*, where two young men in a Corvette chased adventure from town to town. The road stopped being just a way to get somewhere and became a stage where the American story played out with all its grit and glamour.

The Day the Road Was "Improved" to Death

Ironically, Route 66's success helped kill it.

In 1956, the Federal-Aid Highway Act launched the Interstate system—high-speed, limited-access freeways designed to get you from Point A to Point B faster, straighter, and with fewer stoplights and pie breaks. Mile by mile, new interstates like I-55, I-44, and I-40 began to swallow up sections of the older road or bypass its main streets entirely.

To a family in a hurry, the interstates were a blessing. To the towns that had grown up hugging the edges of 66, they were a slow-motion disaster. Traffic thinned. Motels emptied. The neon buzzed for fewer and fewer cars each year.

By June 1985, the government made it official: U.S. Route 66 was decommissioned from the federal highway system. The famous shield came down as a national route number, replaced by local and state designations—or, in some cases, nothing at all.

For many communities, it felt like being erased from the map.

Ghosts, Diehards, and a Second Life

But here's where the story takes a very Route 66 turn.

Instead of disappearing, the old road refused to stay buried. Travelers—first a trickle, then more—started seeking out the "Historic Route 66" signs that appeared in some states. They wanted the slower, quirkier version of America that the interstates skipped: the café with cracked vinyl booths, the service station turned into a tiny museum, the motel that still handed you a real metal key.

Grassroots groups sprang up: state Route 66 associations, preservation societies, and local tourism boards determined to save what was left of their Main Street of America.

Pieces of the old highway were nominated as National Scenic Byways and, in some stretches, elevated to All-American Road status—the highest honor a scenic highway can get.

The rest of the world caught on. Travelers from Europe, Asia, and beyond flew into Chicago or Los Angeles just to drive this legendary route they'd seen in movies and heard about in songs. Vintage cars started showing up at gas stations that had been quiet for decades. Tourism dollars followed, giving some struggling towns a new lifeline.

Meanwhile, pop culture kept adding fresh coats of paint. Disney and Pixar's movie *Cars* reintroduced a whole generation of kids to the idea of a fading highway packed with stories worth saving. Books, documentaries, and photo essays multiplied. If the 1950s had been the first golden age of Route 66, this was a second, stranger one—half nostalgia, half revival.

A Road with a Birthday

As Route 66 reaches its 100th year in 2026, the spotlight is back on the Mother Road in a big way. Congress passed the Route 66 Centennial Commission Act in 2020, creating an official body to help plan and promote celebrations, preservation projects, and educational efforts for the centennial.

Lawmakers have also pushed to designate Route 66 as a National Historic Trail, a move aimed at protecting the route and boosting the economies of communities along its roughly 2,400-mile length. Museums and state organizations are gathering oral histories from people who grew up on the road, patrolled it as troopers, waited tables at its diners, or piled into station wagons for summer vacations along its curves.

In other words, the story of Route 66 isn't over—it's being actively told, remembered, and, in some places, rebuilt.

A Century-Long Conversation

So what do you do with a road that started as a practical short-cut, carried the heartbreak of the Dust Bowl, fueled postwar dreams, nearly died of "progress," and came roaring back as a world-famous icon?

You celebrate it.

You tell the stories of the people who argued over its number in a smoky meeting room, then spent years pushing to get it paved.

you remember the families who followed its white lines west with everything they owned tied down under tarps. You tip your hat to the waitresses, mechanics, motel owners, and sheriffs who kept watch over those long miles of asphalt and concrete. You honor the preservationists who refused to let the lights go out.

This book is part of that celebration—a snapshot of Route 66 at the century mark. We'll zoom in on the wild facts, the strange landmarks, the endangered treasures, the legendary diners, the tall tales, and yes, a few shadows along the way.

Because a road doesn't become "the Mother Road" just because someone wrote it on a sign. It earns that title one story at a time.

And now, a hundred years after its birth on a map, Route 66 is still inviting you to add yours.

Cyrus Avery: The Man Behind the Mother Road

If Route 66 is the "Mother Road," Cyrus Avery is the man who decided where the family would live.

He was not a professor or a politician in a marble building. He was a businessman in Tulsa who had stared at too many muddy roads and dead-end towns and thought, "We can do better than this." Avery made his money in oil and real estate, but his real

obsession was simple: good roads bring good business.

As cars started to take over American life, Avery watched the same story repeat. Where the roads were bad, farms struggled, small towns stayed poor, and travelers did not linger. Where the roads were good, stores opened, gas pumps appeared, and downtowns lit up at night. He joined the Good Roads movement, ran for local office, and picked up a nickname on his campaign material: "Tulsa County's Original Good Roads Man." That was exactly how he wanted people to see him.

So when a national highway system was being planned, Avery did not sit quietly. On the federal board that was drawing lines on the map, he argued hard for a Chicago to Los Angeles route that would swing south through Oklahoma instead of skimming past it up north. In his mind, that diagonal line meant opportunity. Every town it touched could hang out a shingle, build a café, pump gas, rent a room, and catch some of the money moving across the country.

He did not just help shape the route and pick the number 66. He also helped organize the U.S. Highway 66 Association, a group of business owners and boosters who treated the highway like their shared storefront. They ran ads, held promotions, and pushed for paving because they believed every smoother mile meant more travelers stopping in their towns instead of simply passing by somewhere else.

Avery called Route 66 the "Main Street of America" for a reason. He pictured a road that did not sneak around communities, but ran right through them. In his mind, a gas station, a tourist court, and a family diner were not side effects. They were the point. Good roads would revive local business, keep small towns alive, and give ordinary people a chance to make a living serving whoever rolled in next.

Most travelers today will never hear his name. They will just remember the neon vacancy sign, the friendly person behind the counter, and the feel of an old two-lane under their tires. But every time a mom and pop shop sells a slice of pie along Route 66, you can see what Cyrus Avery was working toward.

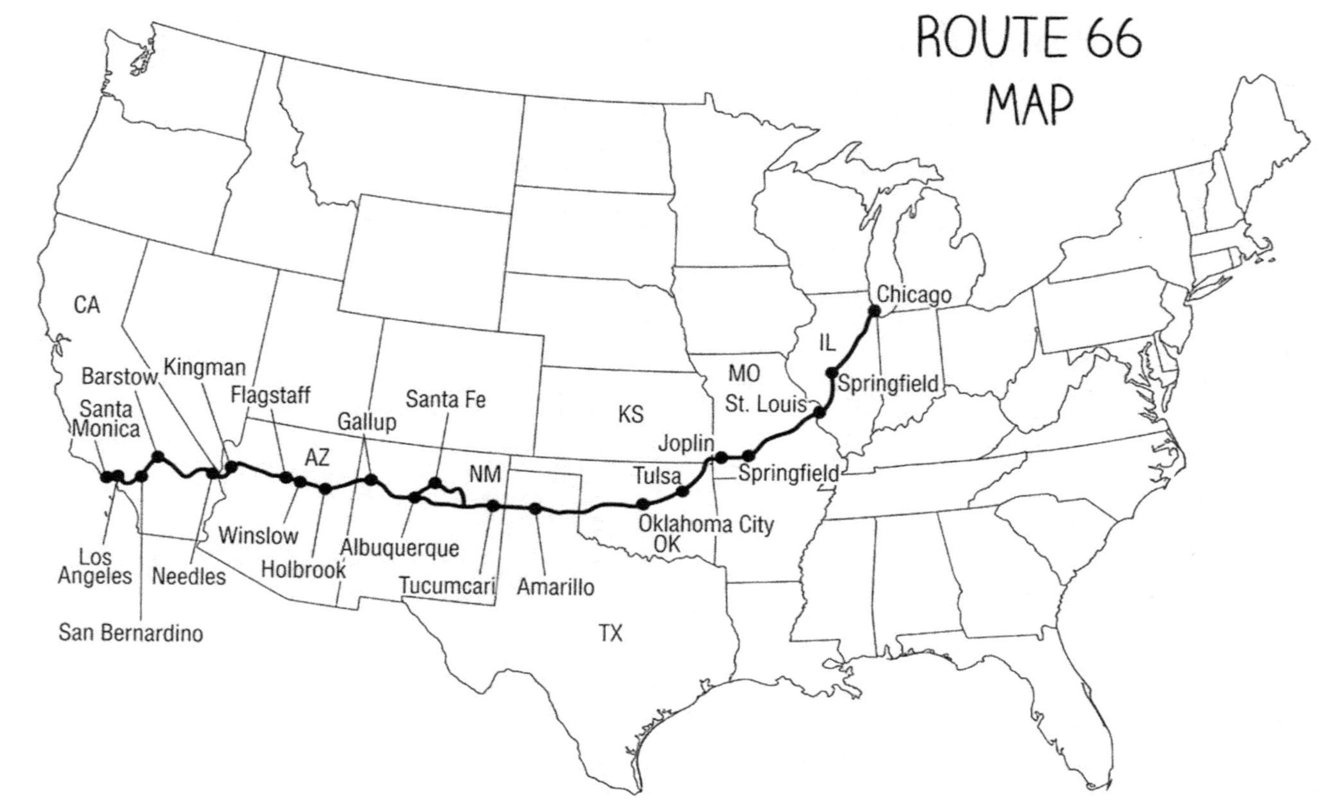

ROUTE 66
MAP
Chicago
IL
Springfield
MO
St. Louis
KS
Joplin
Springfield
Tulsa
Oklahoma City
OK
Amarillo
TX
NM
Santa Fe
Tucumcari
Albuquerque
Gallup
Flagstaff
AZ
Winslow
Holbrook
Kingman
Barstow
Needles
Santa Monica
Los Angeles
San Bernardino
CA

Chapter 2

CRAZY FACTS AND A BIT OF TRIVIA ABOUT ROUTE 66

Eight states, three time zones, one road.

Route 66 runs about 2,448 miles from Chicago, Illinois to Santa Monica, California, crossing eight states and three different time zones along the way.

Kansas got only 13 miles... and made the most of it.

The entire Kansas stretch of Route 66 is just about 13 miles long, yet it squeezes in three historic towns: Galena, Riverton, and Baxter Springs. That tiny slice is also one of the only sections that never needed to be realigned from its original 1926 path.

The "longest stretch" of Route 66 has three winners.
New Mexico has the most total miles, **Oklahoma** has the longest drivable section today, and **Arizona** preserves the longest uninterrupted stretch of the original road.

When it "opened," big chunks were still dirt.
In 1926, only about 800 miles of Route 66 were paved. The rest was gravel, brick, or plain dirt. It took another eleven years before the road finally became fully paved.

There is a stretch that once played "America the Beautiful."
Near Tijeras, New Mexico, engineers cut special grooves into a section of old Route 66. If you drove exactly 45 mph, the rumble strips would "play" part of America the Beautiful through your tires. Over the years the grooves have worn down and the song has faded, but the idea hasn't. Route 66 associations across several states are now working to bring musical highway sections back to the Mother Road. Stay tuned.

World's largest concrete totem pole is just off 66.
In Totem Pole Park near Foyil and Chelsea, Oklahoma, you can visit a 90-foot concrete totem pole built with tons of cement, steel, sand, and rock. It started as one man's art project and ended up as one of the strangest Route 66 icons.

A grandfather built a giant blue whale for his grandkids.
The famous Blue Whale of Catoosa, Oklahoma began as one man's private playground for his grandchildren. He sketched a whale, kept going, and ended up with a concrete

creature about 20 feet tall and 80 feet long that now draws visitors from all over the world.

Route 66 helped launch the Golden Arches.

The site of the first McDonald's restaurant stands in San Bernardino, California, right off Route 66. The original building is gone, but the spot is now a museum packed with fast-food memorabilia and Mother Road history.

Heritage tourism in the "Route 66 states"

A broader 2015 analysis of heritage travel in the **eight Route 66 states** estimated at least **$14.5 billion** in related spending—Route 66 heritage is a big slice of that pie.

Annual direct Route 66 spending

A Rutgers economic study estimated **$132 million per year** in *direct* Route 66-related spending, including **$38M in tourism, $67M in Main Street businesses,** and **$27M in museums** along the corridor.

You literally drive across an earthquake zone.

Route 66 crosses the San Andreas Fault at a place called Blue Cut in California's Cajon Pass. Drivers cruise over one of the most famous fault lines on earth without even realizing it.

Texas kept almost all of its original 66.

In the Texas Panhandle, roughly 90 percent of the original Route 66 alignment is still in use. You can roll through classic towns and roadside stops on pavement that has been carrying traffic since the early days.

Giant fiberglass spacemen guard the route.

Those towering "Muffler Men" along Route 66, like the Gemini Giant in Wilmington, Illinois, are 18 to 30-foot fiberglass figures originally built as roadside ads. Some now hold rockets instead of mufflers and have become Route 66 celebrities in their own right.

You can sleep in a concrete teepee.

At Wigwam Motel locations along the route, travelers still check in to individual concrete teepees, often with vintage cars parked at each door for photos. It is weird, charming, and one of the most photographed overnights on the entire road.

The one-lane "Sidewalk Highway" that carried cross-country traffic

In northeastern Oklahoma between Miami and Afton, an original 1920s stretch of Route 66 survives that is only about nine feet wide. Locals nicknamed it the "Sidewalk Highway" because when two cars met, both drivers had to drop a wheel into the dirt to pass. It looks like somebody poured a narrow driveway straight across the prairie, yet it once handled full national highway traffic.

They seriously planned to nuke a new road near 66

In the early 1960s, engineers cooked up "Project Carryall," a proposal to use twenty-two nuclear explosions to blast a new railroad cut and a section of future I-40 through the Bristol Mountains in California, just north of Route 66. The plan went as far as detailed engineering reports before people started asking if maybe blowing up part of the desert with atomic bombs for a shortcut was a terrible idea.

The "Devil's Highway" was a child of Route 66

For years, one of 66's spurs was signed as U.S. Route 666. It got that number simply because it was the sixth branch off 66, but the "666" freaked some drivers out and turned the signs into high-theft souvenirs. Between the spooky stories, the crash legends, and the stolen markers, highway officials finally gave in and renumbered it U.S. 491, though road geeks still call it the Devil's Highway.

A ghost light that lines up with old Route 66

Near the Oklahoma–Missouri border, not far from 66, people have reported a mysterious floating light for more than a century on what locals call Spooklight Road. The glowing orb drifts, splits, and disappears on clear nights, and there are all kinds of ghost stories to explain it. Skeptical investigators eventually showed that under the right conditions you are probably seeing distant car headlights on an old stretch of Route 66 refracted in the night air, but most visitors still prefer the haunted version.

A hidden POW camp sat in a cotton field off 66

During World War II, an ordinary cotton field near McLean, Texas, just off Route 66, became a camp that held around 3,000 German prisoners of war. They worked nearby farms, played soccer, and even made handicrafts that locals bought, all inside barbed-wire fences only a short walk from the Mother Road. Today the camp is gone, replaced again by fields and a small historical marker, so most travelers pass without any idea that an entire wartime village once stood there.

A Route 66 ghost town was bought by a chicken-chain founder

The near-abandoned town of Amboy, California, with its classic Roy's Motel and Café sign, sits out in the Mojave along Route 66. In the 2000s it was so empty it briefly went up for sale online. Restaurant entrepreneur Albert Okura, founder of the Juan Pollo chicken chain and owner of the Original McDonald's Museum on Route 66 in San Bernardino, bought the whole town. His stated goal was to keep Amboy frozen as a 1950s time capsule and use it to draw travelers and promote both Route 66 and his chicken.

Part of old Route 66 is literally under a lake

South of Springfield, Illinois, an early 1930s alignment of Route 66 followed Cotton Hill Road toward Glenarm. When the city dammed Sugar Creek in the 1930s to create Lake Springfield, the rising water swallowed that alignment, including its bridge. You can still hike old pavement through the woods until it vanishes into the lake, and during severe droughts pieces of brick and roadbed have even reappeared out of the water.

One of 66's oddest museums is dedicated to barbed wire

In McLean, Texas, travelers find the Devil's Rope Museum, which is almost entirely about barbed wire, the stuff that fenced off the Old West. Inside are thousands of different wire patterns, fencing tools, "war wire," and barbed-wire art. Tucked into the same building is a Texas Route 66 museum with vintage signs, motel relics, and even a giant cow, so you can walk in for Mother Road nostalgia and walk out an accidental expert on fences.

Cadillac Ranch has a weirder little cousin made of VW Bugs

Near Conway in the Texas Panhandle, a playful tribute to Cadillac Ranch appeared in 2002: five battered Volkswagen Beetles buried nose-down in the dirt beside old Route 66. Travelers began calling it **Slug Bug Ranch** (sometimes simply Bug Ranch), and like its Cadillac counterpart, visitors were encouraged to spray-paint the cars.

For years the colorful Beetles greeted travelers near Conway. Recently, however, the installation was relocated to **Amarillo**, where it now stands along Interstate 40 near Starlight Ranch. The tradition continues—spray paint in hand—as the ever-changing VWs keep the Mother Road's quirky roadside spirit alive.

Trivia:

In what year was U.S. Highway 66 officially established as part of the numbered highway system?
Answer: 1926

What is the classic total length of Route 66, in miles, from Chicago to the Pacific coast?
Answer: 2,448 miles

? Before it was extended to Santa Monica, Route 66 originally ended in which major California city?
Answer: Los Angeles

? Which famous novelist gave Route 66 the nickname "the mother road" in a 1939 book?
Answer: John Steinbeck, in *The Grapes of Wrath*

? What small Texas town proudly calls itself the "Midpoint of Route 66," exactly 1,139 miles from both Chicago and Los Angeles?
Answer: Adrian, Texas

? Which U.S. national park is the only one that contains a signed section of historic Route 66 inside its boundaries?
Answer: Petrified Forest National Park (Arizona)

? At just over 7,200 feet above sea level, the highest point on historic Route 66 sits at the Continental Divide in which state?
Answer: New Mexico

? Which U.S. president signed the 1956 Federal-Aid Highway Act that led to the Interstate system that would bypass much of Route 66?
Answer: President Dwight D. Eisenhower

? At the western end, the "official" terminus of Route 66 in Santa Monica is at the intersection of which two streets?
Answer: Olympic Boulevard and Lincoln Boulevard

In what year was U.S. Route 66 officially removed (decommissioned) from the federal highway system?

Answer: 1985

Roughly how many buildings, bridges, and road segments along Route 66 are listed on the National Register of Historic Places today: around 25, 75, or more than 250?

Answer: More than 250

What 1946 song, written by Bobby Troup, helped make the road world-famous with the line "Get your kicks on Route 66"?

Answer: "(Get Your Kicks on) Route 66"

Which 1960s television show followed two young men driving a Chevrolet Corvette and often used Route 66 as its backdrop?

Answer: *Route 66*

Which animated movie about talking cars introduced a new generation to a fictional Route 66 town called Radiator Springs?

Answer: *Cars* (Disney·Pixar)

Route 66 is best known by two big nicknames. One is "The Mother Road." What is the other?

Answer: "The Main Street of America"

Through how many states does historic Route 66 travel, and what are they?

Answer: Eight states: Illinois, Missouri, Kansas, Oklahoma, Texas, New Mexico, Arizona, and California.

Which city in Missouri proudly calls itself the "Birthplace of Route 66"?

Answer: Springfield, Missouri.

Which Oklahoma city has been officially designated the "Capital of Route 66"?

Answer: Tulsa, Oklahoma.

What nickname is often given to Cyrus Avery for his role in planning and promoting Route 66?

Answer: The "Father of Route 66."

What is the historic nickname "Will Rogers Highway" referring to?

Answer: It is another nickname for U.S. Route 66, honoring humorist Will Rogers.

In downtown Chicago, on which street do travelers find the longtime "Begin Historic Route 66" sign?

Answer: Adams Street, just west of Michigan Avenue.

Near what large body of water does Route 66 begin at its eastern end?

Answer: Lake Michigan.

Many travelers think of a famous pier as the symbolic end of Route 66, even though the legal terminus is inland. What pier is that?

Answer: The Santa Monica Pier.

What two basic colors were used on the classic U.S. Route 66 highway shield?

Answer: Black and white.

Which small Texas town built its identity around being the exact midpoint of historic Route 66, 1,139 miles from each end?

Answer: Adrian, Texas.

Which city in Arizona is famous for its "Standin' on the Corner" park that ties together Route 66 and the Eagles' song "Take It Easy"?

Answer: Winslow, Arizona.

What nickname was often used during the Dust Bowl years for many migrant farm families who traveled west along Route 66, especially from Oklahoma?

Answer: "Okies."

Which famous roadside art installation just west of Amarillo, Texas, features classic Cadillacs buried nose-first in the ground?

Answer: Cadillac Ranch.

The fictional town of Radiator Springs in the movie *Cars* was inspired in part by real communities along Route 66. Which Arizona town is most often mentioned as a key inspiration?

Answer: Seligman, Arizona.

What towering green fiberglass "astronaut" stands guard over Route 66 in Wilmington, Illinois, and has become a favorite photo stop?

Answer: The Gemini Giant.

Chapter 3

THE GRAPES OF WRATH EFFECT

Picture a loaded truck on a two-lane highway. Mattresses tied to the roof. Kids wedged between crates of tools and battered suitcases. Oklahoma dust still clinging to the tires. That is the image John Steinbeck burned into the world's memory in *The Grapes of Wrath*.

Before his book came out in 1939, Route 66 was important, but it was mostly a practical road. It was the shortest all-weather route from the Midwest to California. Truckers used it. Farm families used it. People knew it as "66" or as a federal highway number on a black and white shield. Locals already understood it was a lifeline, but outside the region it did not have much myth attached to it.

Steinbeck changed that.

He and his wife had driven west along 66 in the late 1930s and seen the real migrant camps, the roadside garages, and the worn-out cars. In *The Grapes of Wrath*, he turned that experience into the journey of the Joad family, who lose their Oklahoma farm and head for California along Highway 66. He did not treat the road as background. He treated it almost like a character.

In an interlude chapter he writes, "Highway 66 is the main migrant road." Then comes the line that Route 66 would never escape: "66 is the mother road, the road of flight." With those words, he gave the highway its most famous nickname and its defining role. It was not just pavement any more. It was the path of desperate people running from drought, debt, and dust toward the hope of work and dignity.

The book hit like a thunderclap. It won the Pulitzer Prize. It was attacked, banned, and burned in some places. It was also read by millions. A year later, John Ford's film version took those same images and put them on gigantic screens. Now audiences who had never been within a thousand miles of Oklahoma or the Mojave Desert could picture Route 66 as the road crowded with overloaded cars, grieving families, and tired eyes watching the horizon.

After *The Grapes of Wrath*, Route 66 was never just "that diagonal highway from Chicago to Los Angeles" again. It became a shorthand for the Dust Bowl migration, for "Okies" in search of work, for the hard side of the American dream. Any time a photographer wanted to say "struggle" or "hope on the move," they pointed their lens at an old 66 bridge or a long straight stretch of road disappearing into the heat haze.

That reputation stuck. When boosters later promoted Route 66 as a tourist route, they borrowed Steinbeck's language. Signs, museums, and guidebooks started using "Mother Road" as if it had always been there. Preservation groups quoted *The Grapes of Wrath* to argue that the road was not just concrete that could be replaced, but a piece of American story that needed to be saved.

The funny thing is, many people who drive Route 66 today have never read the book from cover to cover. They might only know a quote, a movie scene, or a general impression of poor families in old trucks. Still, that shadow travels with them. When they see an abandoned gas station leaning in the wind or a faded tourist court sign, they do not just think "old building." They feel, even if they cannot explain it, that this road once carried people who were betting everything on one more mile.

In that sense, Steinbeck did two big things for Route 66. He gave it a name that stuck in the national imagination, and he froze a specific moment of its history in place. Long before neon, rock-and-roll, and vacation road trips, he showed 66 as a hard road for people in crisis. Later generations layered on new meanings, but the Mother Road he named still has that serious core underneath the souvenirs.

So when you see "Mother Road" on a sign or a T-shirt, you are hearing an echo from Chapter 12 of a novel published in 1939. One writer looked at a busy highway full of broken-down cars and frightened families and decided the road itself deserved a title. The country agreed. And Route 66 has been living with that name, and that story, ever since.

Chapter 4

HOLLYWOOD GOES ON THE ROAD

Bobby Troup

Songwriter, "(Get Your Kicks on) Route 66"

Before the road had a theme song, Bobby Troup and his wife

Cynthia packed up their green 1941 Buick convertible and headed west, chasing his dream of writing music in Hollywood. They

picked up Route 66 near Chicago and followed it all the way to California, watching the place names roll by in a rhythm of their own. Somewhere between the road signs and the long stretches of two-lane blacktop, Cynthia tossed out a line: "Get your kicks on Route 66." Bobby ran with it. By the time they reached Los Angeles, the bones of the song were in his head, and soon Nat King Cole would turn their road trip into one of the most famous travel tunes in history.

When: 1946

Ride: Green 1941 Buick convertible

Clark Gable

"King of Hollywood"

Clark Gable did not just glide from set to set. He was a road guy. During the 1940s, he checked into Boots Court Motel in Carthage, Missouri, a sleek little motor court planted right on Route 66. Local history says he first stayed there in 1942 while traveling on a war-bond tour, then came back again after the war, choosing a modest room with a carport over any marble-floored palace. Today, travelers still request "his" room, just to sleep where the most famous leading man of his day once dropped his bags for the night.

When: 1942 and 1947 (visits recorded at Boots Court)

Ride: Private car, pulled right into the motel's individual carport

Gene Autry

The Singing Cowboy

Before country music award shows and giant arenas, Gene Autry was crisscrossing the country as "The Singing Cowboy," radio star and movie hero. Route 66 was one of his working highways, and before Hollywood made him a legend he even worked as a railroad telegraph operator in Chelsea, Oklahoma, along the Mother Road's corridor. In Missouri, Boots Court's old guest lists and local stories point to Autry as one of their marquee visitors, parking under the same neon that still glows there today. Imagine pulling in after a long day's drive and realizing the cowboy on your kid's lunchbox had slept just a few doors down.

When: 1940s touring years

Ride: Touring car with band and gear in tow

Mickey Mantle

Baseball legend,
New York Yankees

Route 66 runs through Mickey Mantle country. He grew up in Commerce, Oklahoma, just off the Mother Road, and his name still shows up on Route 66 memorials and tour stops there. As he rose from small-town kid to Yankees superstar, Mantle traveled the route and, like other celebs of the day, turned up on the guest list at Boots Court in Missouri. Today, tour buses stop near his statue and memorial, and baseball fans chase both history and hot pavement on the same road he once knew as home.

When: 1940s–1950s, especially his early pro years

Ride: Team and personal cars along his home stretch of 66

Elvis Presley

*The King of
Rock and Roll*

In 1956, a young Elvis Presley rolled into Springfield, Missouri, to play a show at the Shrine Mosque. Instead of staying at the town's fancy hotel, stories say he argued with his manager, walked down the road, and checked himself into the more down-to-earth Rail Haven Motel on Route 66. Room 409 is still preserved today as the "Elvis Suite," filled with memorabilia and mid-century flavor. It is a reminder that for at least one night, the King picked a classic motor court on the Mother Road over luxury.

When: May 17, 1956

Ride: Touring car (the motel keeps the room, not the keys)

Marilyn Monroe

Icon of Hollywood's Golden Age

Marilyn Monroe's name floats through Route 66 lore like neon reflected in a puddle. Along the western reaches of the highway, several classic properties claim her as a guest. In Kingman, Arizona, the historic El Trovatore Motel lists her among its early celebrity visitors, and today you can book a Marilyn-themed room under the same long sweep of neon that once pulled in passing movie stars. Other spots near the California end of 66, like the Georgian Hotel in Santa Monica and the Sycamore Inn, also tell stories of Marilyn dining or staying just a short hop from the Mother Road.

When: 1940s–1950s (golden age travel years, often remembered as local legend)

Ride: Studio cars and chauffeured sedans, long before GPS told anyone where to turn

James Dean

Rebel, racer, and forever young

James Dean is more myth than man now, and Route 66 leans into that myth. Historic motels along the highway, like El Trovatore in Kingman and the Blue Swallow in Tucumcari, feature James Dean murals and themed rooms. Local histories say he stayed at some of these spots while crisscrossing the Southwest during his brief career, the same years he was racing cars and filming the movies that made him iconic. Today his image leans against painted roadsters on motel walls, watching over the stream of travelers chasing their own restless road stories.

When: Mid 1950s

Ride: Sports cars and studio vehicles; his Porsche Spyder often appears in Route 66 mural art

Jimmy Stewart

*Everyman hero
with a Route 66 address
for the night*

Jimmy Stewart is the last person you picture as "Hollywood fancy," which is why he fits El Rancho and Route 66 so well. During the classic western era, he stayed at the El Rancho Hotel in Gallup while filming in the surrounding desert. The hotel now has a Jimmy Stewart room, so guests can literally sleep under his nameplate and old movie stills.

It is easy to imagine him wandering the lobby in the evening, tall and quiet, while trucks and family cars rolled past on Highway 66 outside. For one more night, everyone in town shared the same road and the same front door.

When: 1940s–1950s filming years

Ride: Studio cars and production vehicles routed through Gallup on Route 66

Rita Hayworth

Screen siren in a cow-town lobby

Rita Hayworth was pure Hollywood glamour, but even she needed a real bed between scenes. Local histories and the El Rancho's own star lists put her among the hotel's guests. Today there is a Rita Hayworth room at the hotel, and travelers still request it just to say they stayed "in Rita's place" on the old Mother Road.

Think about the contrast. Outside, dusty pickups and family sedans are parking under neon. Inside, one of the most famous faces of the 1940s is checking in at the front desk. That mix of cattle country and movie stardust is exactly what makes Route 66 fun.

When: 1940s golden age years

Ride: Studio transportation and location cars arriving on Route 66

Gregory Peck

Atticus Finch with a room key

Gregory Peck, who later became the calm moral center of *To Kill a Mockingbird*, was also part of the Route 66 story. El Rancho's guest history includes him among the stars who lived at the hotel while westerns were being shot all over the nearby mesas. His name is now on one of the rooms, framed by vintage photos and wood beams.

You can picture him leaning over a script at a small desk, while just outside the window you would have heard big American sedans, work trucks, and buses humming along Highway 66. Serious actor on the inside, roaming road on the outside. Classic combination.

When: 1940s–1960s location shoots

Ride: Film company vehicles and star cars traveling the Route 66 corridor

Mae West

"Come up and see me" on 66

Mae West brought her larger-than-life attitude to a very real place on Route 66. She shows up on the El Rancho's long list of star guests, and today her name is on one of the vintage rooms overhead. Guests joke that checking into the Mae West room feels like stepping into one of her punchlines, only with creaky floors and a neon glow outside.

It is a fun mental picture. Route 66 cowboys and traveling families downstairs, and upstairs a comedy legend settling in after a day of filming. The same highway that served truckers and tourists also delivered some of the sharpest wit in movie history.

When: Mid twentieth century Hollywood travel years

Ride: Studio limos and production cars coming in on Route 66 from California

Doris Day

America's sweetheart with a menu item

Doris Day's connection to Route 66 shows up in a tasty way. The El Rancho's restaurant and lounge in Gallup serve items named for some of their famous guests, including a Doris Day cocktail on the menu. Her name also appears in lists of stars who stayed and dined at the hotel while filming nearby.

So you can sit at a table off the old highway, order something with her name on it, and look around the same dining room where she once ate between scenes. Outside, semi trucks and road-trippers still follow the Mother Road. Inside, the soundtrack has not really changed that much.

When: 1940s–1960s film and travel years

Ride: Studio transportation and cast cars using Route 66 as the main east–west line

Kirk Douglas

*Tough guy checking
into a Route 66 castle*

Kirk Douglas spent part of his career riding Route 66 to work. When westerns were filming around Gallup, New Mexico, he stayed at the El Rancho Hotel, the big stone lodge that sits right on the highway. His name is now one of many on the walls and doorplates upstairs, where each room honors a different Golden Age star.

You can picture him stepping out of a studio car, squinting into the New Mexico sun, and walking straight from the Mother Road into the wood and stone lobby. For modern travelers, sleeping in "his" hotel feels like sharing a set with one of Hollywood's toughest leading men.

When: 1940s–1960s filming years

Ride: Studio transportation and film caravans rolling in along Route 66

Errol Flynn

Swashbuckler in cowboy country

Errol Flynn is famous for swords and sailing ships, yet he also has a footprint on Route 66. During location shoots in the Gallup area, he used the El Rancho as a home base just like the other western stars of his day. His name appears on guest lists and in hotel lore, and many stories picture him trading his pirate boots for cowboy dust between scenes.

Imagine a traveler pulling into the same parking lot in a family sedan while Flynn is upstairs running lines for his next close-up. That mix of high adventure and small-town highway life is exactly the kind of contrast Route 66 does best.

When: 1940s–1950s location shoots

Ride: Studio cars and production trucks that followed Route 66 to the sets

Jack Benny

*Radio royalty on
a road-trip stage*

Jack Benny spent years entertaining America on radio and early television, so it is only fitting that he also turned up along its most famous road. He appears on El Rancho's list of star guests, one more name in the long roll of Hollywood royalty who slept just a few steps from Highway 66. You can almost hear him turning the lobby into an impromptu stage, squeezing a joke out of a missed wake-up call or a dusty drive.

For guests today, spotting his name on the wall is a reminder that the same road that carried long-haul truckers and vacationing families also delivered one of the sharpest deadpan comics of all time.

When: Mid twentieth century touring and filming years

Ride: Studio and tour cars traveling the Mother Road between gigs

Guy Lombardo

*Big-band leader
with a boat at
a drive-in*

Boots Court in Carthage, Missouri, has its own celebrity roster, and one of the most colorful entries belongs to bandleader Guy Lombardo. He is remembered not only for staying and dining there, but for a famous photo of his sleek boat parked at the adjacent Boots Drive-In. The image looks like something out of a movie: polished boat on a trailer, neon and burgers in the background, Route 66 just beyond.

It is a perfect snapshot of the era. Dance music on the radio, big bands touring the country, and a motor court that could host both a celebrity and his boat on the same strip of blacktop.

When: 1940s–1950s touring years

Ride: Touring car and boat in tow, pulled off to rest along Route 66

Oprah Winfrey + Gayle King

TV royalty on a girlfriends' road trip

In 2006, Oprah and her best friend Gayle King set out to "see the USA in a Chevrolet," filming a cross-country adventure from California to New York. Somewhere between karaoke sing-alongs and deep-dish pizza, they rolled off the interstate and onto old Route 66 for the real thing—diners, neon, and small-town charm. One of their most famous stops was Mr. D'z Route 66 Diner in Kingman, Arizona, where they ordered burgers, fries, and the house caramel root beer. Oprah loved it so much she later had cases shipped to her studio audience.

For a new generation, that one episode did what a thousand travel brochures couldn't: it showed that Route 66 wasn't just nostalgia for old-timers—it was still a living, driveable slice of Americana worth leaving the freeway for.

When: 2006 cross-country "Oprah & Gayle's Big Adventure"

Ride: A Chevrolet road-trip car, loaded with cameras, snacks, and two best friends

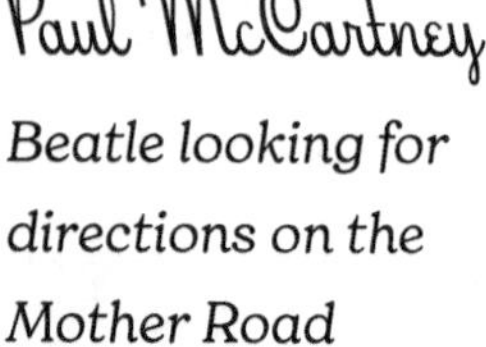

Paul McCartney

Beatle looking for directions on the Mother Road

In August 2008, travelers on a quiet Oklahoma county road got the surprise of a lifetime: a man in a car pulled over, rolled down his window, and asked if he really was on Route 66. The driver turned out to be Paul McCartney, on a low-key American road trip. Word of the encounter spread quickly among locals and Route 66 fans. Today, a roadside sign near Arcadia, on an original stretch of the highway, marks the spot where the ex-Beatle briefly stopped to make sure he was still following the Mother Road.

It's a tiny moment, but a perfect Route 66 story: no red carpet, no entourage—just one of the world's most famous musicians, squinting at a map and asking directions like any other lost traveler.

When: August 2008 road trip through Oklahoma

Ride: A modest road-trip car, quietly cruising historic Route 66 backroads

Disney-Pixar's Cars – A Route 66 Inspiration

Disney-Pixar's *Cars* (2006) may be an animated film about talking vehicles, but it's also a loving tribute to Route 66 – its towns, people, and history. The movie's fictional setting, Radiator Springs, was directly inspired by real Mother Road communities that faded after the highway was bypassed. In fact, Route 66 historian **Michael Wallis** (author of *Route 66: The Mother Road*) was brought on as a consultant and even gave the Pixar team a two-trip guided tour down Route 66 during early story development. (The filmmakers originally planned to title the movie **"Route 66"** before rights issues led them to rename it *Cars*.) These research road trips immersed Pixar's artists in the lore of the highway and introduced them to its most colorful characters – many of whom found their way, in spirit, into the film.

Radiator Springs is essentially a **composite of classic Route 66 towns**. Pixar's team "gathered" elements from various real locations and legends and combined them into one symbolic small town. For example, the film's neon-lit *Cozy Cone Motel* (run by Sally Carrera) nods to the *Wigwam Motels* of Holbrook and San Bernardino and to the famous **Cozy Dog Drive-In** in Springfield, Illinois – birthplace of the corn dog. Sally's character herself was inspired by a real Route 66 figure: Dawn Welch, the owner of the historic Rock Café in Stroud, Oklahoma (like Sally, Dawn left a city career to run a Route 66 diner). Mater, the rusty but lovable tow truck, was drawn from a **derelict 1951 boom truck** the Pixar crew spotted in Galena, Kansas – a vehicle now restored and proudly displayed in

Galena as "Tow Tater," the real-life Mater. And the peace-loving VW bus "Fillmore" is a tribute to the late **Bob Waldmire**, the itinerant hippie artist beloved along Route 66 (Waldmire's own Volkswagen microbus and free-spirited lifestyle inspired Fillmore's character).

Beyond specific characters and places, *Cars* captured the **emotional truth** of Route 66's story. The film's plot – a once-booming town withering away after being bypassed by an interstate – mirrors the fate of many real Mother Road communities in the postwar decades. In one poignant scene, Sally reminisces about Radiator Springs' heyday, recalling how *"the town got bypassed when the highway went through"* – a dialogue echoing the laments of people like Angel Delgadillo of Seligman, AZ, who actually lived that history. *Cars* conveys an *"impassioned plea"* for those forgotten towns and quirky roadside attractions left **"on the side of the road"** when Route 66 was decommissioned. By anthropomorphizing cars and making the road itself a character, the movie invited a new generation of viewers (kids and parents alike) to feel nostalgia for mid-century American road trips – even if they'd never driven the Mother Road before.

The release of *Cars* in 2006 undeniably sparked **renewed interest in Route 66**. Long-time roadies credit the film with introducing young families to the magic of Route 66, spurring them to take road trips of their own. Almost immediately after the movie, travelers began seeking out the real-life inspirations: little Galena, KS gained fame for its "Mater" truck; the U-Drop Inn gas station in Shamrock, TX (which inspired Ramone's paint shop in the film) saw a bump in visitors; and Seligman,

AZ – often cited as a model for Radiator Springs – welcomed a surge of *Cars* fans eager to meet the "Angel of Route 66" (Angel Delgadillo) in person. Disney even invited many Route 66 folks, like Delgadillo and Dawn Welch, to the film's premieres, acknowledging their contributions to the story. In turn, the popularity of *Cars* helped bolster heritage tourism: children who fell in love with Lightning McQueen and Mater would beg their parents to drive Route 66 for real. The effect was so notable that some have said *"Pixar's Cars saved Route 66"* – at least, it gave the highway a healthy boost in the public eye that continues to this day.

In the end, *Cars* did more than tell a charming tale of animated autos – it **immortalized the essence of Route 66's culture and community** for future generations. By weaving together real landmarks and legends into a heartfelt story, the film honors the Mother Road's legacy. And it's not just an homage; it also delivered a message about slowing down and savoring the journey, a philosophy at the core of Route 66. As Sally says in the movie, *"Cars didn't drive on it to make great time, they drove on it to have a great time."* That sentiment, born from Route 66 wisdom, now reaches millions through *Cars*. The film's success (and its spin-offs like *Cars Land* at Disney California Adventure, a theme park land recreating Radiator Springs) continues to inspire travelers from around the world to hit the real road and discover the **"Mother Road"** for themselves – radiator cap, tail fins, neon signs and all.

Burma Shave

Burma-Shave debuted in 1925 as a Minneapolis brushless shaving cream, but the product didn't break out widely until the company made the highway do the

selling. In 1925–26, sales manager Allan Odell began posting "serial" roadside signs: six small boards spaced about 100 feet apart, each carrying a bite-size line that could be read at speed and only made full sense when the last board delivered the brand name—Burma-Shave.

The trick was narrative momentum. One sign sparked curiosity, the next kept drivers reading, and the final payoff made the name stick. Travelers turned the rhymes into a road-trip ritual—counting boards, guessing endings, and quoting punchlines at diners and service stations. On long corridors—U.S. Route 66 among them—the red-and-white sequences became part of the trip's folklore, later mixing in safety-minded verses without losing the grin.

The business impact was immediate. After an initial $200 investment in signboards, Burma-Shave's business rose to $68,000 in 1927. The campaign then scaled outward until it reached 45 states, with more than 6,000 sign sets installed over 33 years. To keep copy fresh, the company ran annual jingle contests, receiving 50,000-plus entries in some years. By the late 1930s, Burma-Shave was the United States' second-highest-selling brushless shaving cream and appeared in about 17% of medicine cabinets. At its peak the company grossed over $3 million a year nationwide, Today, that would be equal to: $43.8 million. Not bad for a $200 dollar investment.

Chapter 5

LOCAL LEGENDS

Local Legend: Lucille, "Mother of the Mother Road"

Long before there was a fancy roadhouse with her name on it, there was a white two-story gas station sitting all by itself on a lonely stretch of Oklahoma pavement. The pumps were on the ground floor. The home was upstairs. And for almost sixty years, the woman who lived there became one of Route 66's most beloved characters: Lucille Hamons.

The station went up in 1929, just as Route 66 was finding its way across the prairie. In 1941, Lucille and her husband Carl took it over near the little town of Hydro. While Carl hauled freight as an independent trucker, Lucille stayed behind and ran everything else: the pumps, the tiny store, the grill, and a handful of tourist cabins next door.

The years were not easy. She worked through the tail end of the Great Depression, wartime rationing, and the boom-and-bust traffic of the 1950s and 60s. When Interstate 40 finally bypassed her stretch of 66, a lot of businesses simply died. Lucille did not. She kept the doors open, served locals, and greeted the die-hard travelers who still came looking for the old road. Guests remembered her hot meals, her "coldest drinks in Oklahoma," and the way she treated everyone like family.

Somewhere along the way, motorists gave her a new title: "Mother of the Mother Road." The name stuck. Her little station was listed on the National Register of Historic Places, and a neon sign from "Hamons Court" eventually found its way into the Smithsonian as a symbol of mom-and-pop Route 66.

Lucille passed away in 2000, at home, in the apartment above those pumps. Today the building has been restored for visitors, and modern businesses bearing her name keep feeding travelers down the road. But the real legend is still that simple image: a woman in an upstairs window, watching the highway, ready for the next car that needs gas, a sandwich, and a little kindness.

Local Legend: Angel, the Barber of Seligman

If Route 66 has a guardian angel, he cuts hair.

In the tiny town of Seligman, Arizona, a barber named Angel Delgadillo watched the traffic disappear almost overnight when Interstate 40 opened. One day his Main Street chair looked out on a steady stream of cars and buses. The next day, it was mostly tumbleweeds and quiet. Businesses closed.

Friends moved away. People started saying the Mother Road was finished.

Angel refused to accept that.

He kept his barbershop open, even when it did not make much financial sense, and began telling anyone who would listen that Route 66 still mattered. Tourists who wandered off the interstate found a man with a comb in one hand and stories in the other. He talked about the early days, the families, the truckers, the bus tours, and the slow death that came with the bypass. Then he started asking a bigger question: what if the old road could be reborn as "Historic Route 66"?

In the late 1980s he helped organize other business owners and pushed for official recognition of the old highway through Arizona. That effort led to the creation of the Historic Route 66 Association of Arizona and helped spark a preservation movement that spread to other states.

Today, Angel's old barbershop is less a working shop than a preserved piece of Route 66 soul — part museum, part pilgrimage stop, and part living thank-you note to the man who refused to let the road die. Travelers line up for photos, buy T-shirts, and sign guest books from all over the world. On some days Angel still drops by to greet visitors, which somehow makes the whole place feel even more special.

Local Legend: Fran and the Pie at the Middle of the World

If you stand in front of the Midpoint sign in Adrian, Texas, the math is simple. Chicago is 1,139 miles behind you. Los Angeles is 1,139 miles ahead. But for a long time, the real center of Route 66 was inside a low, wind-worn café across the street, where a woman named Fran Houser was rolling out pie dough.

The café travelers know today took shape in Route 66's postwar years, after earlier roadside businesses came and went on the site. Over the decades it changed names and owners as traffic boomed, then faded.

Fran bought it anyway.

Her plan was to run an antique shop. Instead, she found herself behind the counter, serving burgers and baking what became her trademark "ugly crust pies" in a kitchen that looked straight out of Route 66's heyday. The pies were tall, homemade, and a little lopsided, and people loved them. Word spread that there was a woman at the exact middle of the Mother Road who would feed you like family.

Then one day a convoy of cars with longhorns on the hoods pulled up. Out stepped a group from Pixar, scouting locations and people for an animated film about a forgotten highway town. They studied the curve of the café's roof, the old sign out front, and the woman running the place. Years later, when *Cars* hit theaters, Fran recognized herself in "Flo" and her café reborn as Flo's V8 Café.

Today the Midpoint Café has new owners, but the line across the pavement is still there, the sign still declares "when you're here, you're halfway there," and travelers still come in looking for pie and a story. Most of them have heard rumors about a lady named Fran who kept the middle of Route 66 alive with coffee, kindness, and a crust that was never quite perfect, and somehow better for it.

If you are currently somewhere out on Route 66 with a milkshake in your hand, you have my permission to skip this page until after your trip.

Still here? All right. Let us talk about the part of the Mother Road that the postcards do not mention.

I've Seen
De Stubble
Nobody Knows
Keeping Faces Clean
My Job is
Burma-Shave
U.S. 66
The Mother Road

Chapter 6

THE DARK SIDE OF ROUTE 66

"Bloody 66" and roads that bit back

In its heyday, Route 66 was famous, busy, and in many places downright dangerous. Early highway engineers were still figuring things out. Much of the road was two narrow lanes with little or no shoulder, sharp curves, and bridges that felt barely wider than your car. Add overloaded trucks, sleepy drivers, no seat belts, drum brakes, and bald tires, and you had a recipe for trouble.

Certain stretches became notorious. In Illinois and Missouri, locals gave sections nicknames like "Death Alley," "Dead Man's Curve," and "Devil's Elbow." These were not tourist slogans. They were warnings muttered by truckers, highway patrolmen, and small town coroners who saw the aftermath of too many late night crashes. Some curves were so bad that newspapers tracked the body counts and state crews eventually had to rebuild the road just to stop the wrecks.

Nationwide, driving in those days was simply far more lethal than it is now. In the 1920s and 1930s, the United States had a motor vehicle death rate more than ten times higher per mile driven than today. Modern guardrails, traffic engineering, crashworthy cars, and seat belts did not exist yet. People still loved the freedom of the open road. They just paid a far higher price for it.

The danger you could not see on a map

There was another dark side that did not show up on road atlases. For Black travelers, large parts of Route 66 were lined with "sundown towns," communities where they were not welcome after dark and sometimes not welcome at all. Researchers estimate that nearly half of the counties along 66 fell into that category at one time or another.

To stay safe, families relied on the Negro Motorist Green Book, a guide that listed the rare hotels, restaurants, and gas stations that would actually serve them. Planning a simple vacation along Route 66 could mean plotting fuel stops so you did not get stranded at night in the wrong place, carrying extra food, and driving past neon motels that were never really open to you. The same road that symbolized freedom for some came with constant risk and calculation for others.

Murder, mayhem, and true crime on the Mother Road

As if tight curves and quiet prejudice were not enough, Route 66 also collected its share of criminal stories.

Route 66 has always sold itself as freedom: windows down, music up, problems shrinking in the rearview mirror.

Criminals heard that pitch and said, "Perfect."

Because if you're trying to move something you're not supposed to have—or leave somewhere you're not supposed to be—the two greatest inventions in American history are: **a fast car** and **a long road with a thousand turnoffs**. Route 66 didn't create American crime, but it did something quietly helpful for it: it connected big-city opportunity to wide-open space. And in the early days, it did it with fewer cameras, fewer radios, and a whole lot fewer guardrails—literal and legal.

Isolated stretches of highway made easy hunting grounds for robbers and drifters. Over the years there were hold ups at remote gas stations, bodies found in ditches, and a handful of murders that still make the rounds in true crime books and podcasts.

What follows isn't meant to romanticize the bad guys. It's meant to show how Route 66, like every famous stage, attracted more than heroes and honeymooners. Sometimes it attracted men with hats too nice for their job titles, suitcases too heavy for their contents, and a very urgent need to keep driving.

Chicago's "starting line" had a shadow, too

The eastern bookend of Route 66 begins in Chicago, which is basically the perfect place to start a legendary highway... and also a perfect place for a legendary crime era to leave fingerprints.

During Prohibition, Chicago wasn't just loud—it was profitable. And just outside the city, the Route 66 corridor ran through Cicero along Ogden Avenue, a strip that sat uncomfortably close to the orbit of the Chicago Outfit. Whether you're a history buff or just someone who enjoys the phrase "machine-gunned restaurant," Cicero is one of those places where Route 66 and gangland history practically shake hands.

One of the most famous episodes happened in 1926, when Al Capone was headquartered in Cicero and rivals decided they were done sending him angry letters. A caravan of cars rolled past his location and unloaded an absurd amount of gunfire into the building—so much that police later estimated **over a thousand rounds**. The plan, according to accounts of the attack, was to draw Capone and his men toward the windows with an initial distraction, then let the following cars do the rest. Capone survived. A woman in a parked car was injured by flying glass. And Chicago's gang war continued doing what it did best: turning everyday streets into headlines.

The reason this belongs in a Route 66 chapter is simple: Route 66 doesn't only begin in Chicago on a map. It begins in Chicago in *spirit*—and the 1920s had a lot of spirit in the wrong direction.

Joplin, Missouri: "We thought they were bootleggers" (Famous last assumption)

If you want a Route 66 crime story with an actual address and a paper trail, Joplin, Missouri delivers.

In April 1933, **Bonnie and Clyde** and members of their gang laid low in a garage apartment on Joplin's south side. Neighbors got suspicious—too many strange comings and goings, too much noise, the kind of vibe that makes a block watch committee suddenly discover their calling. Authorities organized a raid on April 13, 1933. And here's the detail that feels like it was written by a screenwriter with a dark sense of humor:

Law enforcement reportedly believed they might be dealing with **bootleggers**.

They were not.

A gun battle broke out. Two officers—Detective Harry McGinnis and Constable "Wes" Harryman—were killed. The gang escaped. And in their rush, they left behind undeveloped film that later became some of the most famous candid photos of the Barrow Gang—smirking snapshots that helped cement their legend in the public imagination, even as the body count kept rising.

It's easy to think of Route 66 towns as postcard places—neon, pie, and a friendly wave. Joplin is a reminder that even the friendliest street can become the wrong place at the wrong time when infamous people decide to "rest up" nearby.

Oklahoma City: the kidnapping case that put "G-men" on everyone's tongue

Route 66 doesn't just run through scenery—it runs through major cities, and with cities come bigger crimes, bigger headlines, and bigger law enforcement responses.

In July 1933, oilman **Charles F. Urschel** was kidnapped at gunpoint from his home in Oklahoma City. One of the central names tied to the case was **George "Machine Gun" Kelly**. The investigation drew intense attention, including from FBI Director J. Edgar Hoover, because federal kidnapping law had recently changed and this was exactly the kind of high-profile case that could either redeem the Bureau's reputation or embarrass it.

It became a landmark moment in American crime history: major investigation, national coverage, multiple arrests and convictions, and a public that suddenly realized criminals could be hunted across state lines by people who did not have to ask permission to keep chasing.

And that's the Route 66 connection again: when roads link regions, criminals can move faster—but so can consequences.

Route 66 was never just a road for vacations. It was a road for *movement.* And movement, for better or worse, is oxygen for big stories.

The Welch Family Murders (1961)

Four boys in a tent. Two parents in a car. One night that still haunts Route 66.

Most Route 66 "dark stories" feel like campfire material—spooky, exaggerated, and safely distant.

This one isn't.

In early June of 1961, James (J.D.) and Utha Welch were traveling west with their four young sons, doing what families had done on the Mother Road for decades: chasing sunshine and a better season ahead. Instead of a motel, they chose a simple roadside campout near Seligman, Arizona. The boys slept in a small tent. Their parents stayed in the car nearby.

Sometime during the night, someone approached the parked vehicle and shot both James and Utha at close range. The boys didn't wake up. The desert, wide and quiet, swallowed the sound.

Morning brought the kind of moment that permanently changes a life. The children walked over expecting sleepy parents and breakfast plans, and instead found both of them dead in the front seat. Confused and terrified, they tried to flag down help on the highway until motorists finally stopped and authorities arrived.

The case shook people for a reason: it wasn't a bar fight, or a criminal deal gone bad. It was a family, asleep on a famous road, in open country that should have felt safe. Investigators chased leads and suspects, and a name emerged that many believed fit the pattern—but the case never ended with the clear, satisfying conclusion most people expect when something this brutal happens.

That uncertainty is part of what keeps the story alive. Not as entertainment. As a warning and a weight.

Route 66 is neon and nostalgia, yes—but it's also miles of lonely darkness between towns. The Welch murders are one of the hardest reminders that the Mother Road carried more than dreamers. It carried danger too, and sometimes it parked right beside a family who never saw it coming.

A "fun" detour: when Hollywood checked in... and something else checked in too

Speaking of folklore that's clearly labeled as folklore—Route 66 also collected ghost stories the way it collected bumper stickers.

One of the most famous is **Hotel Monte Vista** in Flagstaff, Arizona (right on the Mother Road's corridor). The hotel has long leaned into stories of strange happenings, including a "phantom bellboy" reported by guests. And yes—this is where the John Wayne story shows up.

According to the hotel's own long-told account, **John Wayne** experienced the "phantom bellboy" during stays there and described the presence as friendly. No, this isn't court evidence. It's not a police report. It's not a confession signed by Casper.

But it *is* a well-known piece of Route 66 lodging lore tied to a real place, a real celebrity, and a hotel that's been telling the same story for years.

And honestly? After you've driven enough miles on old alignments, listened to enough wind slap a motel sign, and watched enough headlights cut through desert darkness, you don't need to believe in ghosts to understand why people start telling ghost stories.

Why tell the dark stories at all?

So why shine a black light on such a beloved highway?

Because it makes the picture honest. Route 66 has always held both neon and shadows, joy rides and white knuckles, friendly diners and locked doors. Knowing about the wrecks, the sundown towns, and the unsolved crimes does not ruin the magic. It reminds us that every "good old days" memory sits on top of real people's losses and hard lessons.

When you roll down the Mother Road today in a car with airbags and anti lock brakes, guided by GPS and stopping where you please, you are enjoying a privilege that earlier generations on 66 did not have. This little "do not read until after your trip" chapter is here so that, when you pull off under a glowing neon sign tonight, you will feel not only the nostalgia but also the weight of the history under your wheels.

Top Route 66 Attractions (Chicago to ʃanta Monica)

Experience the best of the Mother Road! Below we've organized 200 must-see Route 66 stops by category – Museums, Diners, Motels, and Roadside Attractions – all of which are still standing and ready to welcome travelers. Each entry lists the name, location, and a short witty description highlighting why it's worth a stop. Buckle up for a fun tour of Route 66's quirkiest icons, tastiest eats, retro sleeps, and roadside wonders.

A Customer
We Hate to Lose
At 60 per
A Curve
Don't take
Burma-Shave
U.S. 66
The Mother Road

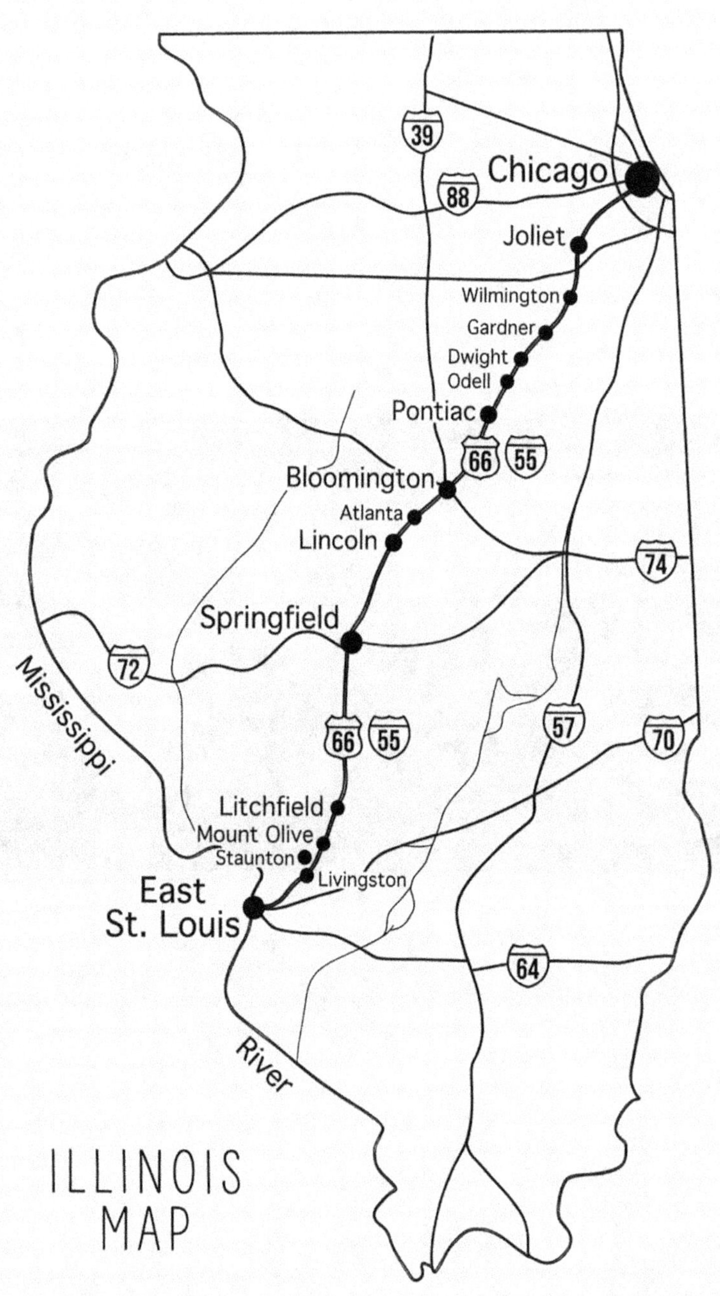

39
88
Chicago
Joliet
Wilmington
Gardner
Dwight
Odell
Pontiac
66 55
Bloomington
Atlanta
Lincoln
74
Springfield
72
66 55
57
70
Litchfield
Mount Olive
Staunton
Livingston
East
St. Louis
64
Mississippi
River
ILLINOIS
MAP

Chapter 7

ILLINOIS

Welcome to Illinois, the proud starting line of Route 66 – where the Mother Road gets roaring with a Chicago swagger and a Midwestern grin. Here, a single turn of your wheels takes you from the canyons of Chicago's skyscrapers to the whisper of cornfields downstate. Illinois wears many hats: one is a fedora tilted over Chicago's eyes (channeling a bit of Al Capone mischief), another is a seed cap out in the farming heartland waving at you from a tractor. The moment you hit the Chicago lakefront — whether you begin at the longtime downtown sign or the city's new centennial marker at Navy Pier — you know you're in for a journey.

But don't think for a second this state is all business. Illinois has a quirkier side that'll have you grinning before you even hit Missouri. This is the land that gave the world the **Cozy Dog**, a.k.a. the original corn dog on a stick - yes, we deep-fried pure genius in batter and called it roadside cuisine. It's also a place where **giant legends** wave howdy: a 30-foot tall **Gemini Giant** spaceman guards a diner, a **Paul Bunyan** statue hefts a gargantuan hot dog in Atlanta, and a massive ketchup bottle water tower looms in Collinsville for no reason other than we like big condiments. Consider these oversized oddities our way of keeping you entertained: Illinois knows a road trip should be fun. One minute you're biting into deep-dish pizza in Chicago, the next you're cruising past a towering fiberglass spaceman in a tiny town – it's all part of the show.

Illinois is mighty proud to be the trailblazer for Route 66. We'll happily fill your tank with history (and your belly with pie) before sending you off westward. From Abe Lincoln's old stomping grounds in Springfield to the neon signs of yesterday still glowing in roadside cafes, this state sets the tone: **optimistic**, a touch **irreverent**, and absolutely **welcoming**. Ready to get your kicks in the Land of Lincoln? We thought so. In Illinois, we don't just start your journey – we jump-start it with a wink and a full plate. Onward!

Diners, Drive-Ins & Cafés

- **Lou Mitchell's – Chicago, IL:** The Mother Road's journey starts with a full belly at this legendary Chicago diner. Open since 1923, they hand out donut holes and Milk Duds to guests – because nothing says "welcome to Route 66" like free candy at 7 AM.

- **Dell Rhea's Chicken Basket – Willowbrook, IL:** Fried chicken so famous, it diverted Route 66 travelers off the highway. This 1946 roadhouse serves golden fried chicken in baskets that'll cluck their way into your heart – a crispy, juicy Illinois icon (Colonel who?).

- **Polk-A-Dot Drive In – Braidwood, IL:** A 50's style drive-in splashed with neon polka dots and life-size celebrity statues out front (snap a selfie with Elvis or Marilyn!). Serving classic burgers, shakes, and a side of pure retro kitsch since 1956 – it's a roadside diner you won't forget.

- **Cozy Dog Drive In – Springfield, IL:** Birthplace of the **corn dog** on a stick! Bite into an original "cozy dog" where it all began in 1946. Family-run and full of Route 66 memorabilia, it's a delicious deep-fried history lesson (with mustard).

- **Doc's Just Off 66 – Girard, IL:** Part soda fountain, part Route 66 time capsule. Set in a historic former pharmacy, this old-school stop serves diner classics, shakes, floats, and sweet treats with a strong dose of nostalgia. Settle in, soak up the memorabilia, and enjoy the kind of roadside charm that makes the Mother Road feel beautifully unhurried.

- **The Ariston Café – Litchfield, IL:** One of Route 66's oldest restaurants (open since 1924) serving home-cooked goodness. This classic cafe dishes up fried chicken, pies, and a warm welcome – it's so enduring, it even made the National Register of Historic Places. Pro tip: save room for the homemade baklava, a nod to the founding family's Greek roots.

Museums & Historic Sites

- **Joliet Area Historical Museum & Route 66 Welcome Center – Joliet, IL:** Part history museum, part Route 66 shrine, featuring an immersive exhibit where you "drive" a '60s convertible. Don't miss the Blues Brothers statues on the roof waving you in for a picture!

- **Illinois Rock & Roll Museum on Route 66 – Joliet, IL:** A new museum amplifying Illinois' musical legends along the Mother Road. From Cheap Trick to Chicago blues, it rocks history with a local twist – and yes, it's right on Route 66 (because the highway isn't the only thing that generates some good vibrations).

- **Illinois Route 66 Hall of Fame & Museum – Pontiac, IL:** Jam-packed with Mother Road memorabilia (neon signs, classic cars, even a VW bus), this free museum honors Route 66 legends in a former firehouse · Its like walking into a scrapbook of Route 66 history – complete with stories that'll fuel your road trip inspiration.

- **Pontiac-Oakland Auto Museum – Pontiac, IL:** Classic car buffs, rejoice – this museum showcases gleaming Pontiacs and Oaklands through the ages. It's lovingly curated by a couple who might just give you a personal tour. A perfect chaser after the Route 66 Hall of Fame next door.

- **American Giants Museum – Atlanta, IL:** A new attraction celebrating those enormous fiberglass "muffler men" statues across America. Fittingly located in Atlanta (home of the Hotdog Holding Giant), it displays big statue molds and memorabilia – a **huge** hit for roadside Americana fans.

- **The Mill on 66 Museum – Lincoln, IL:** Once a 1929 roadhouse shaped like a Dutch windmill, now a museum that saved it from *becoming* dust in the wind. This quirky white mill serves up local history with a side of nostalgia (no actual sandwiches, alas).

✳ **Litchfield Museum & Route 66 Welcome Center - Litchfield, IL:** Small-town museum celebrating Route 66 and Litchfield's heritage. Friendly volunteers, vintage gas pumps, and local Mother Road stories make it worth the stop. For the real Sky View nostalgia, head north to the still-operating drive-in itself.

Vintage Motels & Historic Lodging

✳ **Route 66 Hotel & Conference Center - Springfield, IL:** Housed in a former Holiday Inn, it's part lodging and part Route 66 museum. The lobby is filled with Mother Road memorabilia - classic cars, vintage signs, even an Elvis statue. Rooms are standard, but the experience is not: you'll literally be sleeping in a Route 66 exhibit. It's the only hotel where check-in comes with a mini history lesson on the side.

Roadside Attractions & Oddities

✳ **Route 66 Starting Points - Chicago, IL:** The classic downtown kickoff is the longtime "Begin Route 66" sign at Adams Street and Michigan Avenue, where travelers line up for the obligatory first photo. For the centennial, Chicago is also adding a new symbolic starting point at Navy Pier, giving the Mother Road a lakefront send-off worthy of the legend.

✳ **Gemini Giant - South Island Park, Wilmington, IL:** Wilmington's beloved space-age giant no longer stands at the old Launching Pad. After restoration, he was relocated to South Island Park, where the 30-foot astronaut still makes one of Illinois' best Route 66 photo stops. Rocket in hand and helmet gleaming, he remains every bit the road-trip showman — just with a new home.

- **Two-Cell Jail – Gardner, IL:** This teensy 1906 jail has exactly two cells (one for the naughty, one for the naughtier). It once held drunks overnight, but today it holds only curious tourists. Quirky, photogenic, and just steps off 66, it's proof that small-town Americana is alive and well – and sometimes behind bars (at least until the selfie is taken).

- **Ambler's Texaco Gas Station – Dwight, IL:** A beautifully restored 1933 filling station in a quaint town. No fuel sold nowadays, but it operates as a visitor center. It's a prime photo op with its red Texaco star, old gas pumps, and immaculate white and green paint – a pristine reminder of when service stations were cute cottages and attendants wore bowties.

- **Standard Oil Gas Station – Odell, IL:** A tiny 1932 white station with a cheerful red roof, saved from demolition by Route 66 fans. There's a vintage gravity-feed pump out front and often a knowledgeable local volunteer eager to spin tales. Blink and you'll miss it – but stop, and you'll *refill* on some genuine 66 nostalgia (no purchase required).

- **Funks Grove Maple Sirup Farm – Shirley, IL:** A sweet detour where the Funk family has made *sirup* (old-time spelling) since 1824. In summer, buy a bottle of pure maple goodness from their rustic store; off-season, at least get a photo with their woodsy sign. It's a refreshing change of pace on 66 – nature's own candy along the Mother Road.

- **Paul Bunyon Hotdog Statue – Atlanta, IL:** A 19-foot "muffler man" holding not an axe, but a giant **hot dog**. This big guy once advertised a restaurant in Cicero; now he's the beloved mascot of Atlanta. Snap a pic and ponder life's big questions, like *why* a hot dog? (Because Route 66, that's why.) It's bizarre, hilarious, and absolutely awesome – a roadside Americana all-star.

- **Railsplitter Covered Wagon – Lincoln, IL:** Abe Lincoln reads a law book on the "World's Largest Covered Wagon" here This 24-foot tall, 40-foot long wagon (Guinness-certified) sits roadside and makes everyone do a double-take. It's delightfully ridiculous and somehow fitting in the town named after Honest Abe – a giant tribute to a giant figure, log-splitter style.

- **Lauterbach Giant – Springfield, IL:** Yet another muffler man, this one at Lauterbach Tire on Wabash Ave. He proudly waves a huge American flag instead of a muffler. He's been Springfield's patriotic sentry since the 1970s. Drive by and give him a honk or a salute – it's not every day you see a 20-foot tall tire salesman who loves Old Glory.

- **Pink Elephant Antique Mall – Livingston, IL:** A roadside menagerie of giant fiberglass statues: pink elephant (with glasses!), 20-ft tall Atlas holding a donut, a Futuro flying-saucer house, and more. And yes, an antique mall to browse inside, if you can tear yourself away from the photo ops. It's like Route 66's front lawn sale – surreal, sweet, and begging for Instagram glory.

- **Brooks Catsup Bottle Water Tower – Collinsville, IL:** The "World's Largest Catsup Bottle," a 170-ft tall water tower painted like a ketchup bottle from 1949. A roadside landmark that will leave you exclaiming, "Totally worth the condiment-tion!" It's big, it's red, it's bizarre – and it might make you crave a hot dog. Collinsville is a few miles off the 66 track, but this big bottle is legendary Americana, so we'll allow the detour.

West End Service Station – Edwardsville, IL: This restored brick service station once kept Route 66 travelers rolling with gas, repairs, and the occasional cold soda. Reopened in June 2023 as Edwardsville's Route 66 interpretive center, it now shares stories, photos, and souvenirs in a cheerful little time capsule of the Mother Road.

Shavers Grow
Let the little
Take it Slow
Schoolhouses
Past
Burma-Shave
U.S. 66
The Mother Road

MISSOURI
MAP

Chapter 8

MISSOURI

Strap in, friend, because Missouri is about to **show you** why it's called the Show-Me State. If Illinois was the drumroll, Missouri is the opening act, coming in hot with Ozark curves, riverboat charisma, and a healthy dose of **"Oh, you ain't seen nothin' yet!"** Route 66 slices right across Missouri's diverse personality: starting by crossing the mighty Mississippi (wave to the **Gateway Arch** gleaming on St. Louis's skyline) and then dive-barreling into the green hills and hollers of the Ozarks. We Missourians like to brag - quietly, of course - that Route 66 was basically born here. After all, it was in Springfield, MO that a couple of fellas fired off a telegram in 1926 and officially numbered this highway "66," sealing the deal on the Mother Road's name. That's right, our state literally put the 6-6 in Route 66. You're welcome, world.

Now, Missouri's stretch of the Mother Road is like a **crash course in Americana**, delivered with a wink. One minute you might be enjoying a **frothy frozen custard** in St. Louis (Ted Drewes, anyone?), and the next you're cruising over a historic steel truss bridge in a place aptly named **Devil's Elbow**, where the ghosts of truckers past might just ride shotgun. We mix **urban and rural** like a perfect malt: you'll zoom from city neon into winding country two-lanes where limestone cliffs and redbud trees crowd the shoulders. And keep an eye out for our *billboards* – Missouri is famous for them. We'll tempt you with Meramec Caverns signs every few miles ("Jesse James slept here!" they claim) and then, just when you think this state can't get any more offbeat, we invite you to a place called **Uranus**. Yes, you read that right. In our eternal pursuit of making roadtrippers chuckle, we built a faux outlaw town just to declare, in 10-foot-high letters, that the "best fudge comes from Uranus". It's goofy, it's borderline ridiculous, and it's oh-so-Missouri. You'll be laughing and shaking your head – but you'll definitely pull over for a photo.

Through it all, Missouri exudes a kind of friendly, **show-me hospitality**. Locals wave at every stoplight in the small towns. Diners serve pie with a side of tall tales (ask about the time Bonnie and Clyde came through, we love that one). By the time you reach the Kansas state line, you'll have crossed rivers, climbed hills, and maybe left with a free bumper sticker or two ("I ♥ Uranus," anyone?). Missouri's role on Route 66 is the lovable scene-stealer – full of **quirk, charm, and a pinch of rebel spirit**. Consider yourself shown.

Diners, Drive-Ins & Cafés

☕ **Ted Drewes Frozen Custard – St. Louis, MO:** The custard stand so good, it's **always** in season. Try a famous "Concrete," a thick shake so dense they hand it to you upside-down This 1929 roadside institution attracts lines of travelers and locals alike – consider it the coolest brain-freeze on Route 66.

Museums & Historic Sites

* **Route 66 State Park Museum – Eureka, MO:** Housed in a 1935 roadhouse from the long-gone town of Times Beach, it's a "ghost town museum" with Route 66 exhibits. You can almost hear echoes of bootleggers and travelers – and learn why the town literally got wiped off the map (yikes!).

* **Route 66 Museum at the Library – Lebanon, MO:** This cozy exhibit inside the Lebanon public library surprises with a collection of 66 artifacts like old motel registers and cafe tableware. It's low-key and authentic – a little detour to see how a small town saved its Mother Road memories.

* **Route 66 Car Museum – Springfield, MO:** A petrolhead's paradise showcasing 70+ vintage cars, from a 1907 Kiblinger to Herbie the Love Bug. It's the place to drool over classic Corvettes and Batmobiles and imagine cruising 66 in style

* **History Museum on the Square – Springfield, MO:** Springfield proudly claims to be the birthplace of Route 66, and this downtown museum leans into that story with style. Its "Birthplace of Route 66" gallery features interactive neon exhibits, a turquoise '57 Chevy Bel Air, and one of the largest Route 66 timelines and maps in the country.

Vintage Motels & Historic Lodging

- **Wagon Wheel Motel – Cuba, MO:** The oldest continuously operating motel on 66, dating to 1935. These cozy stone cabins are lovingly restored and oozing with charm – park at your door, snap a pic of the glowing neon sign at night, and be part of the living history (rumor has it this motel inspired "Wheel Well Motel" in *Cars*).

- **Munger Moss Motel – Lebanon, MO:** One of Route 66's great neon landmarks, still impossible to miss after dark. The property is in a new chapter and not a dependable overnight stop at the moment, but the marquee remains pure Mother Road theater — the kind of roadside glow that makes travelers slow down, stare, and smile.

- **Rail Haven Motel (Best Western) – Springfield, MO:** Eight original sandstone cabins from 1938 are now part of this Route 66-era motor court. Elvis stayed here in 1956, and today you can book the Elvis-themed suite to honor the King. Classic gas pumps out front and a vintage motel sign complete the time-warp vibe – it's a haven of retro hospitality with modern comfort.

- **Rockwood Motor Court – Springfield, MO:** Nine charming rooms plus a converted filling-station guest room make up this lovingly restored 1929 motor court. Tucked around a small courtyard, it feels intimate, cheerful, and wonderfully human-scaled.

- **Boots Court Motel – Carthage, MO:** Streamline Moderne style at its finest – this 1939 motor court boasts sleek white curves and a radio in every room (as their vintage sign proudly claims). Clark Gable once stayed here, and after a meticulous restoration, you can too. It's "modern" accommodations circa 1940, where neon nostalgia meets a good night's sleep.

Roadside Attractions & Oddities

- **Old Chain of Rocks Bridge – Madison, IL / St. Louis, MO:** A mile-long 1929 bridge over the Mississippi with a curious 22-degree bend halfway. Now pedestrian/bike-only, it's an exhilarating walk with great river views. Stand on the state line painted on the bridge, feel it *sway* ever so slightly, and channel all the Dust Bowl migrants who once crossed this very span into the West. Eerie and majestic, it's engineering meets romance.

- **Gateway Arch – St. Louis, MO:** America's tallest monument – a 630-foot stainless steel arch gleaming on the Mississippi's west bank. Not originally a Route 66 icon but undeniably a must-see in St. Louis. Ride the tram up if you have time, or at least marvel from below at this "Gateway to the West." It's the modern epitome of going westward – fittingly encountered as you venture further on 66.

- **Route 66 Meramec River Bridge – Eureka, MO:** A 1930s bridge that once carried 66 over the Meramec. Closed to traffic now, it's a quiet spot to admire through the fence (a restoration effort is underway). This bridge starred in many family road trip photos back in the day. Even idle, it has a rusting grandeur – a symbol of how pieces of 66 are fighting to outlast the "demise of Route 66".

- **Meramec Caverns – Stanton, MO:** The famous caverns that plastered "See Meramec Caverns" on hundreds of barn roofs across the Midwest. Jesse James supposedly hid out here. Take a cave tour to see formations like the "Wine

Table" and a quirky light show on ancient limestone draperiesOr at least snap a pic by the retro billboards out front. It's classic tourist trap fun – and naturally cool on a hot Missouri day.

- **Murals of Cuba – Cuba, MO:** Cuba proudly calls itself "Route 66 Mural City," and a drive down its Main Street reveals why. Large, colorful murals adorn building walls, depicting everything from the first Model T in town to visits by Bette Davis. It's an open-air art gallery of local history. Park and take a stroll – you'll find quirky shops and the famous **Wagon Wheel Motel** sign along the way, too.

- **World's Largest Rocking Chair – Fanning, MO:** This giant red rocker stands 42 feet tall beside the Fanning 66 Outpost. It held the Guinness title for a while (now second-largest, but still enormous). Climb *into* the chair? Sorry, no – it's for eyes only. But do stop for a photo that will make you look like a doll. The Outpost store nearby offers snacks and Route 66 wine, so you can literally toast to the big chair.

- **Devil's Elbow Bridge – Devil's Elbow, MO:** A picturesque 1923 truss bridge named after a nasty bend in the Big Piney River. Once notorious for logjams (hence the "Devil's Elbow"), now it's a serene spot with a beach below. Drive or walk the one-lane bridge and imagine Model T Fords rattling across. The scenery here – bluffs, forest, gentle water – shows why early travelers fell in love with the Ozarks.

- **Uranus Fudge Factory – St. Robert, MO:** Prepare to giggle. This faux "town" off 66 leans hard into tongue-in-cheek humor (say the name out loud). Billboards declare "Uranus, Missouri – the *Best* Fudge Comes From Uranus!" Inside the candy shop, staff greet you with "Welcome to Uranus!" It's impossibly silly, deliciously irreverent, and yes, the fudge is genuinely tasty. Don't leave without visiting the sideshow museum and shooting range – Uranus has it all.

- **Gillioz Theatre – Springfield, MO:** A stunning 1926 movie palace just a block off Route 66 in downtown Springfield. Its marquee lights up Park Central East like it's still the Jazz Age. If you can't catch a show, at least admire the ornate façade and vertical sign. It's one of those historic gems that whisper of glamorous nights gone by – and it's part of the lifeblood of a city that calls itself the "Birthplace of Route 66."

- **Gary's Gay Parita – Ash Grove, MO:** A lovingly recreated 1930s Sinclair gas station that became a legendary unofficial stop. The late Gary Turner would greet everyone with a smile and a story. Although Gary's passed, his family keeps the place up as a tribute. Vintage pumps, signs, and old cars set the scene – it's like stepping onto a 1930s postcard. Stop in and experience the spirit of Route 66 friendship (and maybe sign the guestbook).

- **66 Drive-In Theatre – Carthage, MO:** One of the last operating drive-in movie theaters on Route 66. Its 66-foot screen and retro marquee transport you to 1955 on a warm summer night. Catch a flick under the stars if timing permits. If not, at least pull in for a daytime peek – it's wonderfully preserved, down to the playground in front of the screen. Good old-fashioned American fun lives here.

- **Red Oak II – near Carthage, MO:** An "artificial" ghost town created by artist Lowell Davis. He moved and rebuilt old buildings (general store, school, garage) from decaying Red Oak to this site. Stroll the gravel lanes to see vintage tractors, a Phillips 66 gas station, even faux residents (mannequins) sitting on porches. It's free, photo-friendly, and delightfully weird – a love letter to small-town America frozen in time by an artist's vision.

70
Salina
135
335
35
35
Kansas City
Wichita
35
66
Riverton
86
Galena
66
Baxter Springs

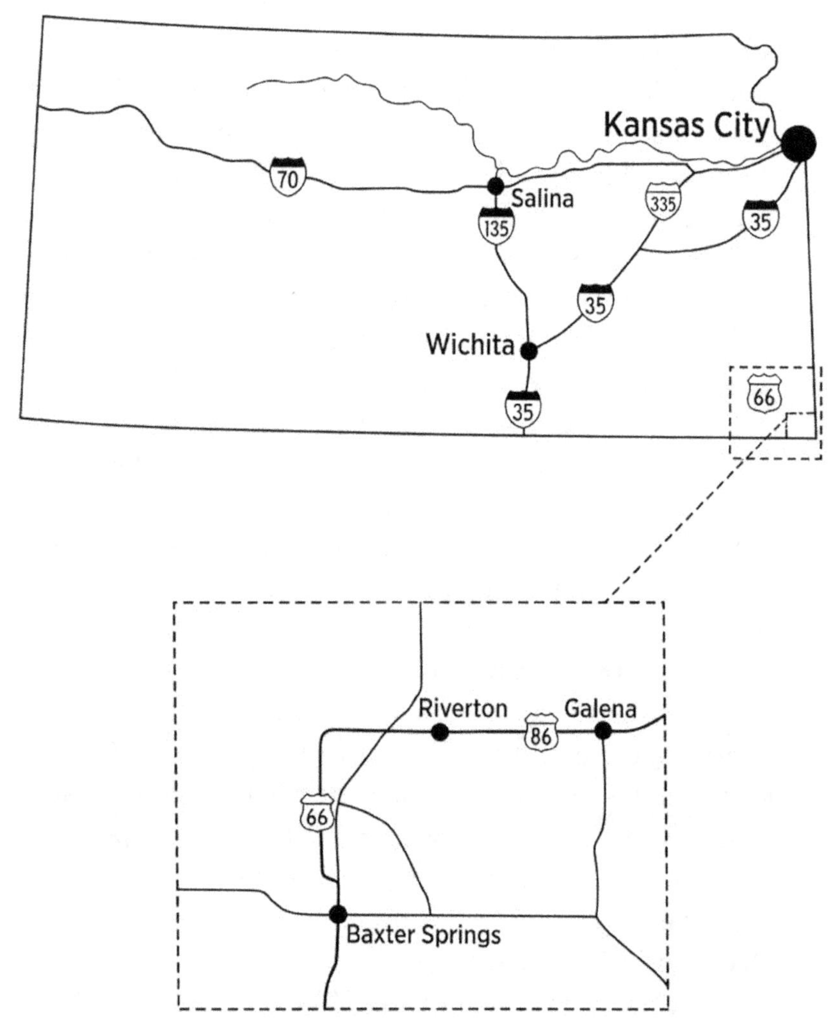

KANSAS
MAP

Chapter 9

KANSAS

Blink and you'll miss it? Not on *our* watch. Kansas may boast the shortest Route 66 stint of any state – a quick **13-mile cameo** across our southeast corner – but oh boy, do we make those miles count. Think of Kansas as the Mother Road's **power nap**: brief, rejuvenating, and surprisingly full of dreams. As you cross in from Missouri, don't yawn or you might drive right through our slice of Route 66 without realizing it. But if you slow down (you've got 13 miles, what's the rush?), you'll find that this little stretch is like a concentrated shot of Americana, served with a friendly Kansas smile. We're the **fun-sized candy bar** of Route 66 states – small, sweet, and guaranteed to lift your mood.

What's in those 13 miles, you ask? For starters, **history and heart** by the bucketful. This is mining country, so you'll see the remnants of boomtown days in places like Galena and Baxter Springs, where old brick buildings and vintage service stations whisper tales of lead and zinc and Wild West lawmen. In fact, Baxter Springs claims to be one of the first "cow towns" in Kansas, and its streets once saw Jesse James and Wyatt Earp (not on the best of terms, mind you). But we're not just peddling history – we've got **whimsy** too. Ever heard of the **Galena "Tow Tater"**? He's a rusty 1951 tow truck with a goofy grin, parked outside a renovated Kan-O-Tex service station. And he's not just any truck – this lovable fella inspired **Mater** from Pixar's *Cars*, putting Galena on the map for Disney fans. Yes, Kansas contributed a key character to the *Cars* universe, which is basically a badge of honor in roadside culture. We do *small-town charm* so well that even Hollywood took notes.

Driving Kansas 66 feels a bit like rolling through a living scrapbook. There's a tidy white **Rainbow Bridge** from 1923 – the last one of its kind – gracefully arching over a creek, perfect for that nostalgic photo-op. There are mom-and-pop diners eager to serve you a slice of pie and ask where you're from (because in Kansas, every stranger is just a friend from out of town). And when you stop in our little communities, don't be surprised if you hear, "Thanks for coming!" more than once. We know you have many miles to go, and we're honored you spent a few of them with us. **Kansas's Route 66** may be the shortest chapter in the Mother Road story, but it's written in bold letters – full of pride, hospitality, and a wink that says, "Good things *do* come in small packages." Consider it a quick hello, a warm goodbye, and a reminder that sometimes the little moments stick with you the longest.

Diners, Drive-Ins & Cafés

- **Cars on the Route (formerly 4 Women on the Route) – Galena, KS:** A restored Kan-O-Tex gas station turned diner, famous for the rusty **Tow Mater** tow truck parked outside that inspired the character in Pixar's *Cars*. Inside you'll find homey sandwiches, home-baked goodies, and likely one of the "women on the route" ready with a story.

- **Nelson's Old Riverton Store – Riverton, KS:** This 1925 general store serves up deli sandwiches and nostalgia in equal measure. Grab a hot "Route 66" sandwich, browse vintage candies, and soak up the old-timey charm – it's like lunching in your grandma's pantry (if Grandma also sold Route 66 souvenirs).

Museums & Historic Sites

- **Galena Mining & Historical Museum – Galena, KS:** Housed in an 1870s train depot, this museum covers Galena's lead-mining boom. It's got mining artifacts, local lore, and a gift shop – plus it's just down the street from Tow Mater (see "Roadside Attractions") for a perfect one-two Kansas combo.

- **Baxter Springs Heritage Center & Route 66 Visitor Center – Baxter Springs, KS:** A 1930 cottage-style gas station turned visitor center. Stop in for a dose of Route 66 hospitality, local history exhibits, and maybe chat with a friendly volunteer about the town's Wild West past.

Roadside Attractions & Oddities

- **"Tow Tater" Truck – Galena, KS:** Outside the Cars on the Route café sits a rusty 1951 boom truck named "Tow Tater". This charming hunk of metal was the inspiration for Tow Mater in Pixar's *Cars*. Kids and adults alike love posing with him. He's dented, he's lovable, and he put Galena on the map. Tell him he's your "best good buddy" and he might not respond – but you'll have a great photo and a warm fuzzy Route 66 memory.

- **Gearhead Curios – Galena, KS:** A restored old service station stuffed with Route 66 memorabilia, oddball finds, and one very big reason to stop: Big A, the towering Texaco-themed muffler man out front. Equal parts souvenir stop and roadside spectacle, it gives Kansas a giant-sized wink before the state's short stretch runs out.

- **Rainbow Bridge – Riverton, KS:** A graceful single-span concrete arch bridge from 1923, the last of its kind on Route 66. This little white bridge has survived 100+ years tucked away on an older alignment. Drive (slowly) or walk over it, and you'll understand why they call it rainbow – its elegant arch reflected in the water is pure magic. A piece of Kansas 66 that's quiet, sweet, and very photogenic.

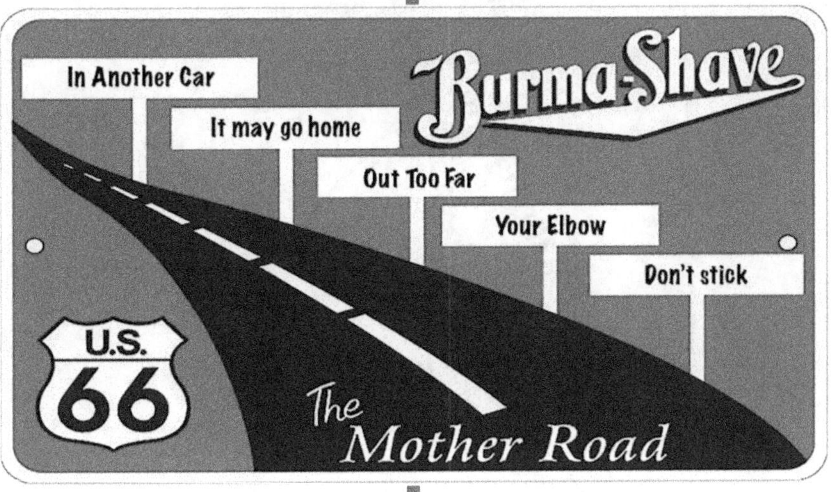
In Another Car
It may go home
Out Too Far
Your Elbow
Don't stick
Burma-Shave
U.S. 66
The Mother Road

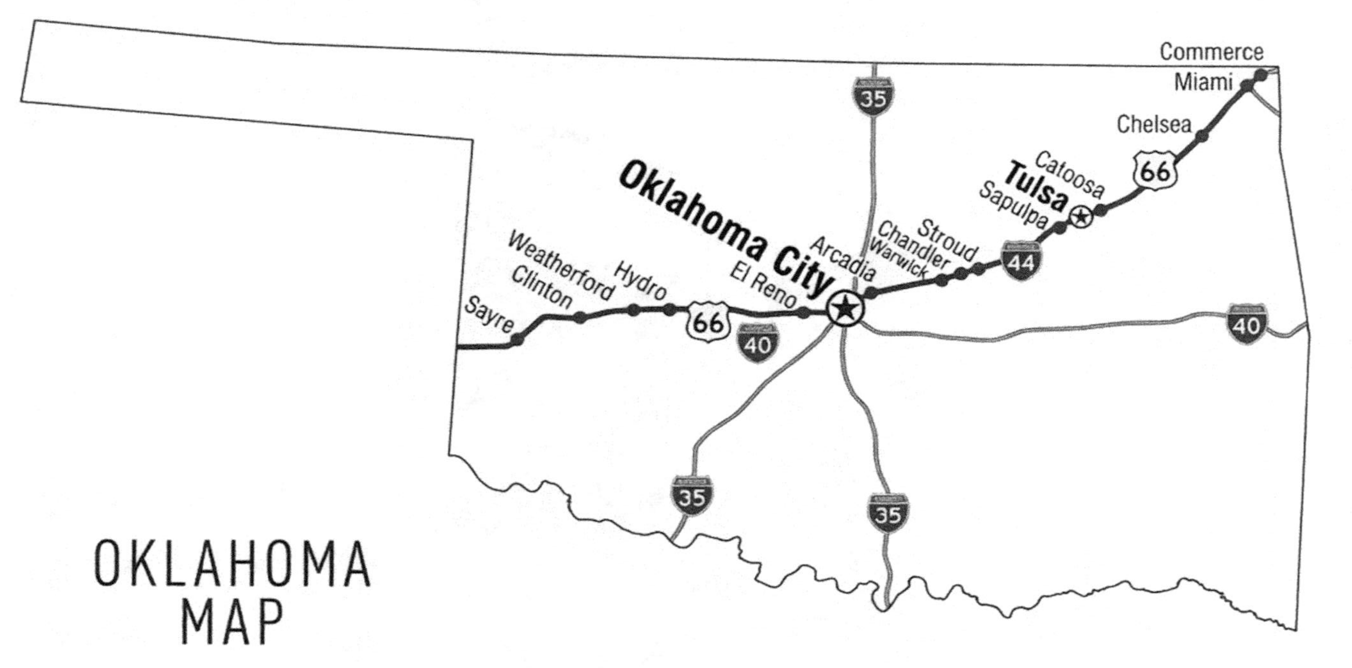

Commerce
Miami
Chelsea
Catoosa
Tulsa
Sapulpa
66
35
Stroud
Chandler
Warwick
Arcadia
Oklahoma City
El Reno
44
40
Hydro
Weatherford
Clinton
Sayre
66
40
35
35
OKLAHOMA MAP

Chapter 10

OKLAHOMA

Y'all ready for some **Oklahoma hospitality**? Hope so, because here in the Sooner State, Route 66 doesn't just pass through – it puts down roots and stays a while. We've got more miles of the Mother Road than any other state (over 400, and we're mighty proud of it) and arguably more classic 66 sights and attractions, too. In other words, Oklahoma is Route 66's home-on-the-range, and we treat it like kin. This is where the highway straightens out across wide-open prairies and small-town main streets, where the locals might greet you like you're long-lost family and the very *road* seems to tell stories at every bend. By the time you cross our border, you'll have learned one of our unofficial state mottos: **"Never met a roadtripper we didn't like."**

Oklahoma's stretch of 66 carries the heartbeat of the highway's history. After all, Tulsa's own Cyrus Avery — born in Pennsylvania but forever tied to Oklahoma — is hailed as the 'Father of Route 66' for good reason. He helped plot this path and insisted it run right through his home state, effectively making Tulsa the crossroads of America. We don't like to brag (okay, maybe a little), but you could say Route 66 was *born* here in Oklahoma's soil and spirit. You'll feel that legacy alive and kicking as you roll along. Tulsa and Oklahoma City show off mid-century architecture and neon signs that still wink at dusk. In Tulsa, you might swing by the famous **Meadow Gold** sign glowing from its own brick pavilion, or cruise 11th Street where classic motels still beckon with buzzing neon cacti. In Oklahoma City, the Mother Road morphs into a big-city boulevard, and east of town the 66-foot soda bottle at **POPS** in Arcadia brings the roadside showmanship right back into view.

We've got **folksy charm** by the truckload. Where else will you find a big blue concrete **whale** smiling at you from a pond? (We built that in Catoosa, just for fun – and it's now one of the Mother Road's most beloved oddballs). Or a **gigantic gasoline pump** towering in Sapulpa? Or how about the ghost of a 1920s filling station attendant waving at you in a preserved station in Chandler? Whether you're grabbing a fried-onion burger in El Reno or browsing Route 66 memorabilia in Clinton's world-class museum, Oklahoma's like that genial uncle who keeps pulling great stories out of his hat. We'll bend your ear about the **Bunion Derby** footrace that came through in '28 (won by an Oklahoman, of course), or how Woody Guthrie sang our Dust Bowl blues as families streamed west on this very road. Every town has a tale, and trust us, we're eager to tell you.

Most of all, Oklahoma offers you **community** on Route 66. Stop in any small town café and someone's liable to say, "Howdy, where ya from? Sit down and eat!" We've kept so much of the old road drivable and lovable – more than 400 miles, in fact – because we believe in it. The Mother Road's part of our family. So as you journey through, from Miami (that's "My-am-uh," thank you kindly) near Kansas to Texola on the Texas line, soak up that friendly, easygoing vibe. Enjoy the red dirt sunsets and the way the wind comes sweepin' down the plain (yep, just like the song). By the time you wave goodbye, you might just agree with Will Rogers that Oklahoma is a place where "strangers are just friends you haven't met yet." And on Route 66, in our neck of the woods, you'll never be a stranger for long.

Diners, Drive-Ins & Cafés

- **Waylan's Ku-Ku Burger – Miami, OK:** Hard to miss the giant yellow cuckoo clock sign! This 1965 drive-in (pronounced "koo-koo") still serves classic burgers, fries, and soft-serve from its cuckoo-themed building. It's quirky, tasty, and one of the last of its kind – truly cuckoo for Route 66.

- **Clanton's Cafe – Vinita, OK:** A down-home diner featured on TV for its chicken-fried steak. Clanton's has been family-owned since 1927, serving comfort on a plate. Try the calf fries if you dare (Google it later) – Anthony Bourdain did! It's old-school hospitality at its best, right on the main street.

- **Tally's Cafe – Tulsa, OK:** A Route 66 landmark in Tulsa's midtown, famous for big breakfasts and bigger cinnamon rolls (seriously, plate-sized!). Tally's glows with neon signage and 1950s charm, and their motto "Be Happy" is literally written on the wall – you'll leave full and, well, happy.

- **Rock Café – Stroud, OK:** A 1939 café built of native rock, beloved for its onion-fried burgers and the indomitable owner who inspired a character in *Cars*. The grill survived a fire and kept on rockin' – just like the Route 66 spirit. Don't miss the jagged "ROCK CAFÉ" neon sign glowing out front

- **POP'S 66 Soda Ranch – Arcadia, OK:** Come for the 66-foot-tall **soda bottle** out front lit by neon bubbles, stay for the 700+ kinds of soda inside. This modern diner/gas station is a fizzy fantasyland – grab a burger and a bizarre soda flavor (peanut butter & jelly pop, anyone?) under that glittering pop-bottle sculpture.

- **Sid's Diner – El Reno, OK:** The onion-fried burger capital of the universe. This tiny 1989 diner gained fame for keeping the old Route 66 onion burger tradition alive – they smash onions into the patty and grill to golden perfection. Greasy, cheesy, and glorious, Sid's proves sometimes the simplest stops are the most satisfying.

- **Route 66 Cafe at the Market – Clinton, OK:** Set in a lovingly reused market building on Route 66, this cheerful Clinton stop serves breakfast and lunch with a side of Oklahoma warmth. It feels rooted in the road rather than dressed up for it.

Museums & Historic Sites

- **Heart of Route 66 Auto Museum – Sapulpa, OK:** Celebrates Oklahoma's car culture with classic automobiles and Route 66 artifacts. The showstopper sits outside:

a **World's Tallest Gas Pump** towering 66 feet high - you literally can't miss it from the road!

* **Route 66 Interpretive Center – Chandler, OK:** Housed in a retro armory, it uses panoramic screens and audio to immerse you in 66's glory days. Kick back in a vintage car seat and watch tales of the road unfold around you – it's part theater, part museum, and totally cool.

* **Oklahoma Route 66 Museum – Clinton, OK:** An official state museum that's a time machine through each era of the Mother Road. Stroll through a 1950s diner, listen to dusty-road ballads, and discover why folks say this is *the* place to understand Route 66's story.

* **National Route 66 Museum – Elk City, OK:** This museum complex celebrates *all* eight Route 66 states. Pose by the giant red VW bug out front, then wander through replica old-time storefronts and vintage car displays – it's like a mini Mother Road village under one roof.

Vintage Motels & Historic Lodging

* **Desert Hills Motel – Tulsa, OK:** A 1953 gem on 11th Street in Tulsa, marked by a giant neon cactus sign that pierces the night. The rooms are simple, the vintage kidney-shaped pool beckons, and the vibe is mid-century cool. Pull in under the porte-cochère and rest easy – you're doing Tulsa like a 1950s roadtripper.

* **Campbell Hotel – Tulsa, OK:** A restored 1927 boutique hotel on Tulsa's 11th Street stretch of Route 66, where jazz-age polish meets Mother Road history. Each room has its own personality, and the whole place feels like proof that

not every great Route 66 stay needs a motor court and a neon vacancy sign.

- **Skyliner Motel – Stroud, OK:** You'll know it by the fabulous neon **"Skyliner"** sign with a shooting star. This small 1950s motel still operates for overnight guests. Rooms are retro cozy, and when that neon star lights up the prairie night, you'll feel like you've discovered a secret slice of American Graffiti along 66.

- **Lincoln Motel – Chandler, OK:** Classic 1939 Route 66 motel with a tidy row of rooms and a neon-lit sign that's been welcoming travelers for generations. It's known for clean comfort and affordable rates – nothing fancy, but when you're road-weary, this little motor court feels like a palace (with your car right at the door, of course).

Roadside Attractions & Oddities

- **Sidewalk Highway (Ribbon Road) – Miami to Afton, OK:** A nine-foot-wide strip of highway – yes, *nine* – from 1922 that you can still drive for a few miles. This one-lane relic (a.k.a. Ribbon Road) taught early drivers the art of cooperation: two cars meeting had to put one set of wheels on the dirt. Taking a bumpy ride on it is like driving on the country's skinniest time machine. Good luck and don't worry – traffic is pretty scarce these days.

- **World's Largest Totem Pole – Foyil, OK:** Ed Galloway's Totem Pole Park boasts a 90-foot concrete totem pole, brightly painted with Native-inspired designs. Built in 1948 as one man's passion project, it towers over a menagerie of smaller totems and a folk art museum (in an 11-sided "Fiddle

House"). It's whimsical, impressive, and a little dizzying to look at – bring wide-angle lens to capture this concrete fever dream.

Blue Whale of Catoosa – Catoosa, OK: A big blue concrete whale smiling in a pond, originally built in 1972 by a husband as an anniversary gift to his wife (now that's love). This kitschy cetacean became a Route 66 icon – you can walk out on its tail, peep into its hollow belly, and fish from its side (locals do!). Recently restored and still utterly endearing, the Whale has *thousands* of fans who stop to say hello – it's the kind of lovable roadside weirdness Route 66 is all about.

Golden Driller – Tulsa, OK: A 75-foot-tall giant oilman standing proudly at Tulsa's Expo Square. He's *not* on 66, but about a mile south – and many roadtrippers swing by to see him. As one of the tallest freestanding statues in the U.S., he's become a symbol of Tulsa. With his hard hat and hands resting on an oil derrick, he's an Instagram hero (and his name is literally on his belt). Big? Yes. Bold? Definitely. Route 66-adjacent? Sure – we'll allow it, because he's just that cool.

Buck Atom's Cosmic Curios – Tulsa, OK: Funky gift shop guarded by "Buck Atom," a 21-foot space cowboy statue unveiled in 2019. Buck wears a cowboy hat and space suit, holding a rocket ship – the newest member of Tulsa's muffler man family. Snap a selfie with Buck and browse the shop's eclectic 66 souvenirs (moon pies, anyone?). It's a stellar blend of retro and modern kitsch – truly taking Route 66 into the final frontier.

- **Cyrus Avery Centennial Plaza – Tulsa, OK:** A riverside plaza honoring the "Father of Route 66," with the striking "East Meets West" bronze showing Avery's Model T beside a horse-drawn wagon. Walk the bridge, take in the skyline, and soak up the moment where Tulsa turns Route 66 history into public art.

- **Meadow Gold Neon Sign – Tulsa, OK:** A restored 1930s sign that once advertised Meadow Gold dairy and now glows from its own brick pavilion along 11th Street. It is one of Tulsa's great neon survivors — less a billboard now than a bright little monument to the city's Route 66 swagger.

- **Blue Dome Building – Tulsa, OK:** A 1924 former gas station crowned with its famous cobalt-blue dome. The building itself gave the Blue Dome District its name, and the surrounding blocks now hum with restaurants, bars, and nightlife. It's a small building with big Tulsa energy.

- **World's Tallest Gas Pump – Sapulpa, OK:** Standing outside the Heart of Route 66 Auto Museum is a giant gas pump 66 feet high. It looms over the landscape like a tribute to every fill-up ever. At night it's lit with LEDs. It doesn't actually dispense 66 feet of gas (thank goodness), but it sure dispenses smiles and great photos. You'll feel *pumped* just standing next to it.

- **Threatt Filling Station – Luther, OK:** A historic 1915 gas station built and operated by an African American family during segregation, offering a safe stop for Black travelers on Route 66. Currently being restored, the little white building with red trim stands as an important reminder of both the adversity and entrepreneurial spirit along 66. You can't go inside yet, but a stop here is a nod of respect to the legacy of the Green Book and those who kept the road open to all.

Arcadia Round Barn – Arcadia, OK: A perfectly round, bright-red barn from 1898 that has become a beloved Route 66 landmark. Its domed loft was ingeniously built to be tornado-resistant (and it's still standing, so it works!). Go inside to enjoy the small museum and great acoustics – sometimes local bands play folk tunes up in the loft. It's a photogenic slice of rural Oklahoma and one *well-rounded* attraction (sorry!).

POP'S Giant Soda Bottle – Arcadia, OK: A 66-foot-tall LED soda bottle sculpture that lights up in rainbow colors at night. It marks the modern POPS Soda Ranch, but the bottle itself has become a Route 66 icon in record time. You can see it from afar, glowing like a neon beacon. It's the most *bubbly* roadside attraction on 66 – and at night, when it shimmers with colors, it simply *pops*.

Milk Bottle Grocery – Oklahoma City, OK: A tiny triangle-shaped building downtown topped by a giant milk bottle on its roof. The bottle has been advertising dairy since 1948 (now it says Braum's milk) and the whole structure is on the National Register. It's the quirkiest 350-square-foot real estate in OKC – a quick drive-by photo and you've got your daily dose of calcium-rich Americana.

Lucille's Historic Gas Station – Hydro, OK: A vintage 1929 two-story gas station (also known as Provine Station) famously run by "Mother of the Mother Road" Lucille Hamons for 60 years. Though long closed, it's preserved on Route 66 with its original porch overhang. Pull over and imagine the days when Lucille pumped gas, fixed flats, and gave advice to travelers like a guardian angel of 66. Her spirit practically inhabits the place – a testament to Route 66 hospitality.

Texola's "No Place Like This Place" Sign – Texola, OK: In the nearly-ghost-town of Texola (pop. a few), one crumbling building bears a hand-painted sign: "There's No Other Place Like This Place Anywhere Near This Place, So This Must Be The Place." Is it a bar? A former diner? Doesn't matter – the cheeky slogan amid Texola's eerie quiet is the real attraction. Snap a pic and appreciate the humor surviving in a town that almost hasn't – this quirky sign is a love letter from the middle of nowhere.

Of Some Guy's Trunk
Pulled Him out
To Him was Bunk
Distance
Proper
Burma-Shave
U.S. 66
The Mother Road

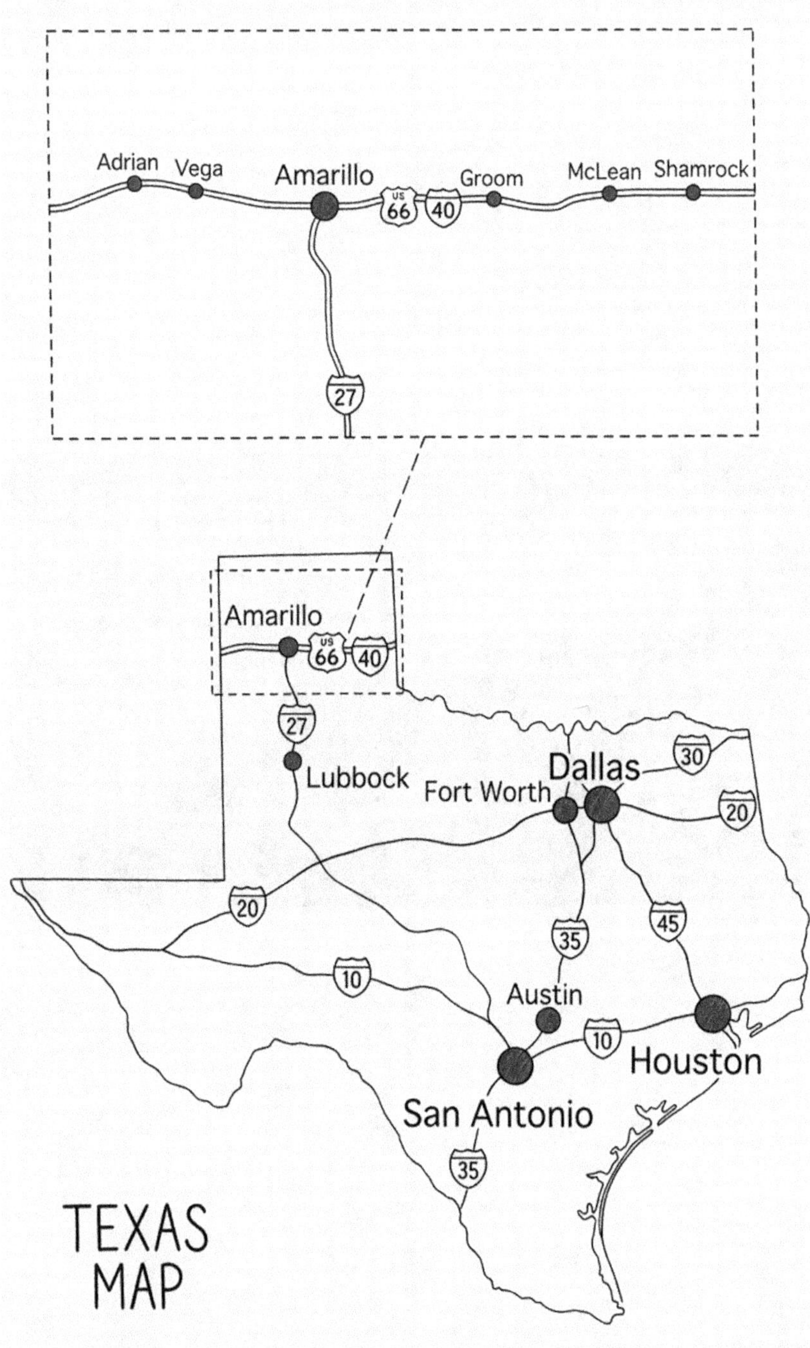

Adrian
Vega
Amarillo
US 66
40
Groom
McLean
Shamrock
27
Amarillo
US 66
40
27
Lubbock
Fort Worth
Dallas
30
20
20
35
45
10
Austin
10
Houston
San Antonio
35
TEXAS MAP

Chapter 11

TEXAS

Howdy, partner – welcome to Texas, where Route 66 might only dip its toes in our Panhandle, but we still do things **bigger than life**. Sure, we've got just about 186 miles of the Mother Road (practically a quick jaunt by Texas standards), but don't you worry – this stretch is pure, grade-A Lone Star spectacle. You're in the land of **big sky and bigger personality** now. Out here, the plains stretch to forever, the steaks are the size of small boats, and the roadside attractions will have you hollerin' "Yeehaw!" before you even hit New Mexico. We Texans like to joke that we could use a little more Route 66 (after all, everything's supposed to be bigger in Texas), but what we got, we absolutely *own*.

As you cruise into Texas from Oklahoma, you'll notice the horizon opening up wide and the smell of adventure (or is that barbecue smoke?) in the air. Route 66 runs straight and true across our Panhandle, peppered with stops that are the stuff of road trip legend. Remember that song "Get Your Kicks on Route 66"? Well, in Amarillo, we prefer "get your **steaks**." Pull up a chair at the world-famous **Big Texan Steak Ranch** in Amarillo, home of the 72-ounce steak challenge – an eating feat so audacious it's free if you can devour the whole slab in under an hour. (And no, that's not a typo – we really mean 72 ounces of beef. In Texas, excess is just another word for dinner.) Even if you're not feeling that carnivorous, you can't miss the atmosphere: giant cowboy boot out front, ranch-style dining hall filled with laughter (or groans from those attempting the challenge), and maybe even a live band twanging in the corner. Everything here is a photo op, including the *huge* rocking chair that makes grown adults look like kiddos.

Moving right along, Texas keeps the hits coming. Ever wanted to make your mark on the American landscape? At **Cadillac Ranch** just west of Amarillo, you can. This isn't a ranch for cattle – it's a pasture for art. Ten classic Cadillacs are half-buried nose-down in the dirt, all tilted at the same jaunty angle, like they dove right into the earth. It's bizarre, it's iconic, and it's 100% Texan in its boldness. Visitors are handed cans of spray paint (or bring your own) to add graffiti to the cars – layers upon layers of neon paint on vintage fins, changing by the hour. Where else but Texas can you create roadside art and be encouraged to leave graffiti? It's an ever-evolving canvas out on the range. Pro tip: you *will* get paint on your shoes, your hands, maybe your dog if he's not careful. Wear it like a badge of honor.

Texas's Route 66 isn't all spectacle, though – it's also a trip through time. In Shamrock, the **Tower Station & U-Drop Inn** rises like an emerald city on the plains, an Art Deco master-piece from 1936 that's so pretty it inspired a building in Pixar's *Cars*. Pull in under that spire and imagine weary 1930s travelers gassing up under the same neon glow. In tiny Adrian, Texas, you'll hit the **exact midpoint** of Route 66 – 1,139 miles from Chicago, 1,139 miles to Los Angeles. There's a cheerful sign and a café with killer pies to celebrate the symmetry. Take a selfie straddling the line; you're halfway to everywhere now. And as you near the New Mexico border, keep an eye out for the **Leaning Tower of Texas** (a deliberately tilted water tower in Groom that'll have you checking if you're seeing things straight) and a field of half-buried VW Beetles known as **Slug Bug Ranch** (because why not one-up the Cadillacs with smaller cars?). We've even got a **giant cross** on the horizon out there, as if to bless your journey west.

In true Texas fashion, our stretch of the Mother Road is equal parts **swagger and soul**. You'll meet some of the friendliest folks in these parts – proud small-town Texans who'll drawl "Howdy, y'all!" at the drop of a hat and tell you to enjoy your stay. So go on, soak it up. Snap those pictures, spray that paint, chow down on that steak (or at least a brisket taco). Texas won't hold you long, but we guarantee we'll leave an impression as big as a Panhandle sky. As we like to say around here, "Drive friendly – the Texas way." And don't be a stranger now, y'hear?

Diners, Drive-Ins & Cafés

Tower Station & U-Drop Inn Café – Shamrock, TX: Dine in an *art deco* masterpiece that looks straight out of a 1936 postcard (because it is). The Tower Station's restored café no longer does full meals, but you can grab a snack or soda in the beautifully preserved green-and-cream interior. By night, the neon lights on its spire will take your breath away – it's like eating inside the Emerald City.

- **The Big Texan Steak Ranch – Amarillo, TX:** Home of the infamous **72-oz steak challenge** – eat it (and all the fixings) in under an hour and it's free! This huge cowboy-themed restaurant is pure Texas kitsch. Even if you're not up for a carnivorous feat, come for the live country music and giant rocking chair out front – everything's bigger at the Big Texan.

- **Golden Light Café – Amarillo, TX:** Since 1946, this unassuming roadhouse on Amarillo's 6th Street (old Route 66) has been slinging greasy-spoon burgers and cold beers. It's also a live music joint at night. Gritty, no-frills and beloved by locals, Golden Light proves that some Route 66 classics shine best in neon and grill smoke.

- **MidPoint Café – Adrian, TX:** Welcome to the exact middle of Route 66! This vintage café celebrates the 1,139-mile mark · with homey vibes and "ugly crust" pies that are downright beautiful to taste. Grab a seat, enjoy a slice, and relish that you're equidistant from Chicago and L.A. – it's all downhill (in a good way) from here.

Museums & Historic Sites

- **Devil's Rope Museum – McLean, TX:** A museum dedicated to barbed wire (yes, really) and Route 66 lore. Experience surprisingly fascinating "devil's rope" history and a side exhibit on vintage highways – proof that even the quirkiest museums can **hook** you in.

Vintage Motels & Historic Lodging

* **Big Texan Motel – Amarillo, TX:** Adjacent to the famed steak ranch, this motel embraces a Wild West theme to the hilt. The facade is styled like an old frontier town, and rooms have saloon doors in the bathrooms. Park your horse (or car) out front and rest up – if you overate at the steak challenge next door, at least your bed is a short "roll" away!
* **Vega Motel – Vega, TX:** More landmark than sure overnight these days, this 1947 adobe-style court remains one of the Texas Panhandle's most evocative Route 66 survivors. The vintage sign and weathered stucco still have that lonely, high-plains magic that makes you pull over even if you're only stopping for a photo.

Roadside Attractions & Oddities

* **Tower Station & U-Drop Inn – Shamrock, TX:** (See earlier diner entry for full description) – *Art Deco gas station/café masterpiece with its green neon tower, now a visitor center.* It's so iconic it even inspired Ramone's Body Shop in *Cars*. Stop by at night to bask in the neon glow; by day, step inside the old café (now info center) to enjoy the 1930s ambiance. Shamrock's pride and joy is a shining example of Route 66 preservation.
* **Leaning Water Tower – Groom, TX:** A water tower deliberately leaning at a gravity-defying angle, as if a giant

tried to tip it over (spoiler: it was a marketing stunt for a now-closed truck stop). It's still standing, slanted, drawing double-takes from I-40 travelers. Pull off at exit 114 and see it up close – trust us, your brain will itch thinking it might fall (it won't). This Tilted Tower of Texas is a prime example of roadside whimsy that makes zero sense and 100% fun.

- **Giant Cross – Groom, TX:** Just down the road from the leaning tower is a 19-story steel cross – one of the largest in the western hemisphere. Surrounded by statues depicting the Crucifixion, it's a spiritual rest stop for many. Whether you're religious or not, you'll be struck by its sheer size and presence. After countless goofy sights, Route 66 reminds you it can do solemn and profound too – everything's bigger in Texas, including the inspiration.

- **Cadillac Ranch – Amarillo, TX:** A public art installation of 10 classic Cadillacs buried nose-first in a row. Visitors are encouraged to spray-paint the cars freely, so they're ever-changing canvases of graffiti. It's an open-air, windswept, paint-scented playground. Bring a spray can and leave your mark on Route 66 (literally) – just be prepared for paint fumes and the possibility that your art will be covered in 5 minutes. Cadillac Ranch is the ultimate interactive roadside icon – equal parts awe-inspiring and oddly poignant as these symbols of American luxury sink into the earth, reborn each day under layers of neon creativity.

- **Slug Bug Ranch – Amarillo, TX:** Cadillac Ranch's cheeky little cousin now lives in Amarillo, where a lineup of half-buried Volkswagen Beetles keeps the spray-paint tradition going. Originally installed near Conway, the bugs have been relocated to a more visible Amarillo home, but the spirit is the same: part art project, part junkyard comedy, part excuse to get paint on your shoes.

- **Route 66 Midpoint Sign – Adrian, TX:** A now-famous sign behind the MidPoint Café proudly declares "Midpoint 66: 1139 miles to Chicago – 1139 miles to Los Angeles". Stand on the "US 66 Midpoint" line on the road, throw your arms out, and grin – you've hit the halfway mark of the journey! Celebrate with pie next door at the café. This is one of those feel-good milestones that embodies the symmetry of the Mother Road – from here on, you're heading "downhill" to the Pacific.

- **Glenrio Ghost Town – Glenrio, TX/NM:** Straddling the state line, Glenrio thrived in Route 66 days, then died when I-40 bypassed it. Today its abandoned gas station, motel, and roadbed provide a haunting glimpse of frozen time. The old postcard-perfect **First/Last Motel in Texas** sign still stands, bullet-riddled but proud. Walk the silent street where only wind and nostalgia blow. It's a poignant pit stop that reminds you why Route 66 is called the Ghost Road in places – but also why efforts continue to keep it alive.

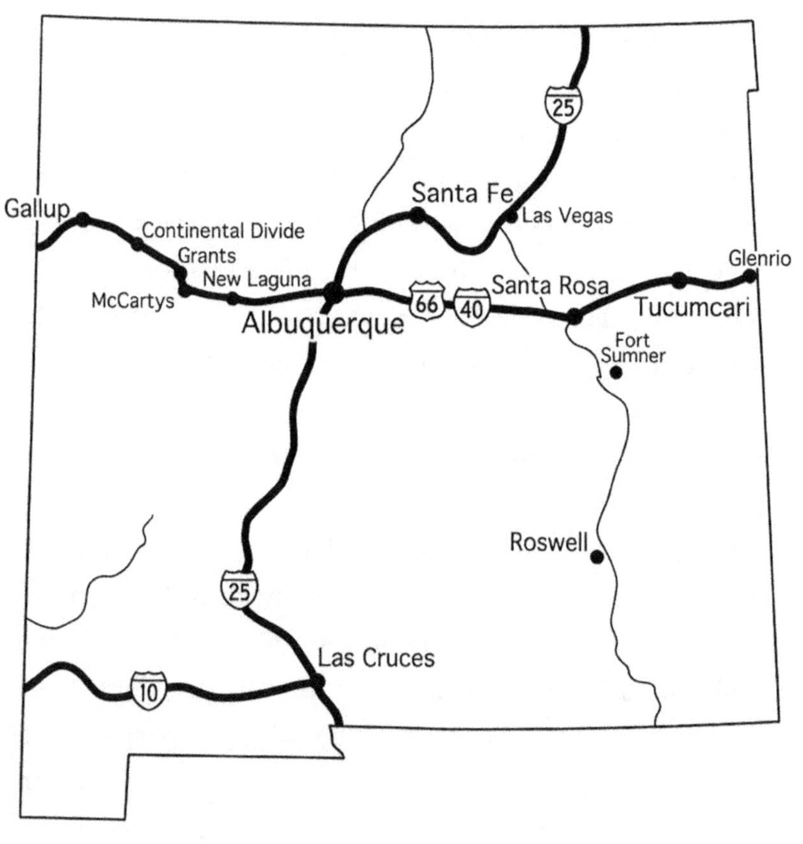

NEW MEXICO
MAP

Chapter 12

NEW MEXICO

Bienvenidos a Nuevo México! Welcome to New Mexico, where Route 66 takes a deep breath of **high desert air** and settles into a whole new groove. Out here, the Mother Road trades the Wild West rowdiness for a bit of Southwest enchantment - and trust us, it's truly enchanting. You're cruising through the **Land of Enchantment**, after all, where every sunset looks like a painting and every diner might just smother your burrito in green chile if you ask nice. New Mexico's stretch of Route 66 is where the road *slows down* and savors the journey. The vibe is part vintage Americana, part ancient pueblo, and part quirky roadside neon dream. It's a place where cultures blend as smoothly as a piñon nut milkshake (yes, that's a thing) and where the official state question is literally "Red or Green?" - referring to chile sauce, of course. We take our chili seriously here, and you'll be asked your preference at least once a day.

(Insider tip: answer "Christmas!" to try both red and green, and you'll get an approving grin from the locals.)

Route 66 rolls into New Mexico from Texas and immediately you sense the change. The horizons stretch further, the air gets drier, and there's a hum of mystique in the wind. In Tucumcari, a town whose very name is fun to say, you'll hit the brakes not for traffic, but for **neon**. Lots of neon. This small city became a big deal on old 66 for its plethora of motor courts vying for travelers' attention with colorful, buzzing signs. "Tucumcari Tonight!" the billboards used to shout – promising 1000 motel rooms. Today, the slogan's still around, and come nightfall the strip is aglow like it's perpetually 1959. The **Blue Swallow Motel**'s sign casts a cool blue buzz on the pavement, the **Tee Pee Curios** shop lights up with its kitschy teepee-shaped entrance, and you half-expect to see a neon-lit cowboy saunter down the street. It's pure magic for neon lovers and anyone craving a time-warp twilight. Grab a malt at a diner, stroll under the blinking signs, and you'll feel like you're in a scene from an old postcard – one that might say *"Greetings from New Mexico, wish you were here!"* (in radiant neon, naturally).

This state's section of 66 is also about **land and legend**. As you drive west, you traverse mesas and sagebrush flats that have hardly changed in centuries. You'll pass through Albuquerque – where Central Avenue *is* Route 66 – and cruise a strip lined with vintage motels, classic Route 66 neon drive-ins, and maybe a few lowriders shining in the sun. Albuquerque gives you a dose of city excitement (old theaters, a university buzz, and diners serving up green chile cheeseburgers as big as the plate), but New Mexico's heart truly beats in the open road and small pueblos beyond. Head toward Santa Fe (on the pre-1937 alignment) if you fancy some artsy charm and adobe architecture – the old route originally looped north to the capital, because even highways knew they couldn't skip Santa Fe's allure. Or stay the course on the later alignment through cut-straight desert to witness the *breadth* of the land. Either way, you're tracing paths that conquistadors, cowboys, and Route 66 cruisers alike have tread. Feel free to let your mind wander as wide as the landscape. Perhaps you'll think about the Dust Bowl migrants who came through seeking a better life under these same endless skies. Perhaps you'll just wonder how that tiny roadrunner bird keeps outrunning your car (they're speedy little guys!).

New Mexico brings the **quirky**, too, have no doubt. You might find a curio shop in Gallup selling both Navajo jewelry and cheesy Route 66 magnets side by side. Or the remnants of a quirky musical stretch near Albuquerque, where specially cut grooves once played "America the Beautiful" through your tires if you hit the speed just right. There's even an 80-foot deep **Blue Hole** in Santa Rosa – a spring-fed pool of astonishingly blue water smack in the desert – where travelers have cooled off for generations. Talk about an oasis! One dip in that 62°F water and you'll be howling (happily) like a coyote. And keep your eyes peeled for roadside art installations, like scrap-metal sculptures of aliens or cowboys that occasionally pop up on the horizon – New Mexicans have a whimsical streak a mile wide. Could be the chile peppers, could be the altitude, who knows?

Ultimately, New Mexico's gift to Route 66 is a feeling – a sense that you've entered a place where **time slows and magic**

seeps in. Maybe it's the ancient pueblos not far from the road, reminding you that people have called this land home long before any highway. Maybe it's the nightly celestial show; our stars do put on a dazzling display out here where city lights are few. Or maybe it's just the warmth of New Mexico's people, a mix of Native, Hispanic, and Anglo cultures all entwined with a shared pride in place. By the time you cross into Arizona, you'll have a bit of enchantment in your soul (and probably a jar of green chile sauce in your trunk). We'll send you off with a hearty "¡Buen viaje!" – happy trails – and don't forget to come back, ya hear? After all, once enchanted, always enchanted.

Diners, Drive-Ins & Cafés

- ☕ **66 Diner – Albuquerque, NM:** Chrome, checkerboard, and cherry cokes – this retro diner on Central Avenue has it all. The waitresses wear poodle skirts, the jukebox plays oldies, and the milkshakes are served in yard-long glasses. Don't leave without trying the famous **Pile-Up** (eggs, hashbrowns, chili, cheese – basically breakfast heaven on a plate).

- ☕ **Frontier Restaurant – Albuquerque, NM:** Not historic Route 66 per se (opened 1971), but a beloved eatery on the Central Avenue strip. This enormous café across from the University of New Mexico is famed for Southwest staples like green chile stew and fresh cinnamon rolls the size of your face. It's open late, always busy, and an Albuquerque icon – consider it a modern Mother Road must-stop for a taste of New Mexico.

Museums & Historic Sites

- **Tucumcari Historical Museum - Tucumcari, NM:** Located in a 1903 schoolhouse, it covers local history from cowboys to Route 66. Out back is a village of old west buildings and even a 1926 caboose. It's a charming time capsule – complete with friendly staff who might just tell you the tale of how **Tucumcari Tonite** became a slogan.

- **Route 66 Auto Museum - Santa Rosa, NM:** Bright red classic cars and hot rods steal the show at this family-run museum. See beautifully restored Chevys and neon signs galore – it's a quick stop just off 66 where horsepower meets nostalgia under one roof.

Vintage Motels & Historic Lodging

- **Blue Swallow Motel - Tucumcari, NM:** The crown jewel of Route 66 motels, in operation since 1939. Park in your very own attached garage, relax on a porch chair, and soak in the glow of the iconic *Blue Swallow* neon sign at night. Lovingly preserved with period furnishings and friendly owners, it's the ultimate "live in a postcard" experience.

- **Motel Safari - Tucumcari, NM:** Retro-cool motor lodge from 1959, updated with mid-century modern flair. Look for the camel on the sign and a vintage Jaguar parked out front. The rooms have a hip vibe (Eames chairs, photos of Elvis), and the hospitality includes fresh "cowboy coffee." It's a stylish slice of Doo-Wop era Tucumcari that still feels fresh.

- **Roadrunner Lodge - Tucumcari, NM:** A 1964 motel reborn with 1960s thematic rooms (want the groovy "1960s

Geek" room, anyone?). Neon roadrunner signs, plush vintage-style bedding, and lawn games in the courtyard make it a fun stop. They even deliver cereal to your room in vintage mini boxes for breakfast. It's half classic, half quirky – 100% memorable.

- **Sunset Motel – Moriarty, NM:** A classic roadside motel from 1959 still run by the same family. The neon sign welcomes you like an old friend, and the rooms have vintage charm with modern touches. Known for its super friendly owners (the grandson of the original builder might check you in), the Sunset proves that mom-and-pop motels on 66 are alive and well – and as hospitable as ever.

- **El Vado Motel – Albuquerque, NM:** A 1937 adobe motor court turned boutique motel, beautifully restored around a courtyard. Mid-century meets modern with stylish rooms, a taproom, food pods, and even a small pool. It's a trendy oasis on West Central Avenue – proof that old motels can be reborn for a new generation of road trippers.

- **Hotel El Rancho – Gallup, NM:** A grand 1937 railroad-era hotel that became "Hollywood's Hotel" for Western movie stars. It has a two-story rustic lobby with a majestic chandelier and autographed photos of John Wayne and Katharine Hepburn on the walls. The rooms boast Navajo textiles and Old West charm. Stay here and you'll feel like a 1940s movie star (spurs not included).

Roadside Attractions & Oddities

- **Russell's Travel Center & Car Museum – Glenrio, NM:** Right at the NM-TX border, this gas station/rest stop surprises with a FREE car museum inside. It's like a mini showroom of American chrome – Corvettes, Bel Airs, muscle cars – plus diner memorabilia, jukeboxes, and vintage signage. Grab a classic burger at the 50s-style diner, then stroll the museum and fuel up on nostalgia (and gas, if needed). It's a modern facility with an old soul, a perfect embodiment of Route 66's enduring appeal.

- **Route 66 Monument – Tucumcari, NM:** A huge stainless steel sculpture titled "Route 66 Monument" (aka "The Mother Road") in front of the Tucumcari Convention Centerroute66times.com. Resembling the tailfin of a '57 Caddy with dual Route 66 shields, it gleams in the sun and is especially impressive at sunrise or sunset. Strike a pose by this 40-foot artwork that screams "Welcome to Tucumcari Tonite!" – it's the town's shiny love letter to the highway that put it on the map.

- **Tee Pee Curios – Tucumcari, NM:** A former gas station-turned-gift shop with a giant concrete teepee as its entrance. Neon "Tee Pee Curios" lettering lights up the night. Outside, there are goofy dino statues; inside, you'll find moccasins, magnets, and maybe even a jackalope or two. It's pure vintage roadside Americana and one of the most photographed storefronts on 66 – quirky, colorful, and utterly charming.

- **Murals of Tucumcari – Tucumcari, NM:** Tucumcari is mural-crazy, with over 30 public murals splashed across town. Cowboys, classic cars, motel scenes – the town is an open-air art gallery. Don't miss the *Route 66 memorial mural* featuring a map of the highway, or the one of "Blazing Saddles" (yes, the Mel Brooks film). These vibrant works give life to Tucumcari's slogan, "Town of Murals" – a perfect complement to its famous neon.

- **Blue Hole – Santa Rosa, NM:** An oasis in the desert – a natural sapphire-blue spring-fed pool that's 80 feet deep. Route 66 travelers have taken refreshing plunges here for generations, and it's still popular for scuba diving and summer swims. On a sweltering day, nothing beats a dip in the Blue Hole's crystal-clear 62°F water. Even if you just stop to peek, the vivid blue pool will mesmerize you. It's a cool literal *pit stop* that proves Mother Nature can compete with neon any day.

- **Musical Highway – Tijeras, NM:** Once one of Route 66's oddest little party tricks, this eastbound stretch near Tijeras used specially cut grooves to play "America the Beautiful" at 45 mph. The site is no longer reliably signed or fully restored, so think of it as a fading roadside curiosity rather than a guaranteed performance.

- **KiMo Theatre – Albuquerque, NM:** A 1927 Pueblo-Deco movie palace adorned with swirls, thunderbirds, and Southwest motifs. Its flashing neon marquee still beckons on Central Ave. Legends say it's haunted by a friendly ghost. Pop in to see the stunning lobby with Native American designs – it's like stepping into a vibrant pueblo dream. The KiMo is Albuquerque's cultural crown jewel on 66, blending Native artistry with Hollywood glitz.

- **Route 66 Neon Drive-Thru Sign – Grants, NM:** A five-story-tall neon Route 66 shield that straddles the road – you drive right under it like a finish line. At night it glows red, white, and blue, beckoning travelers off I-40 into Grants. It's a new installation with vintage flair, complete with a little tunnel of lights. Roll down the windows, *drive thru the sign,* and bask in the neon glow – it's the closest you'll come to literally driving "through" Route 66.

Continental Divide – Continental Divide, NM: At 7,275 feet elevation, this spot marks where waters flow either to the Atlantic or Pacific. There's a big green sign and a trading post or two. It's a great photo op: one foot on each side of the Divide. No, you won't *feel* different, but it's a neat "I was there" moment. Plus, everything's literally downhill from here – in opposite directions! Talk about a crossroads of the continent.

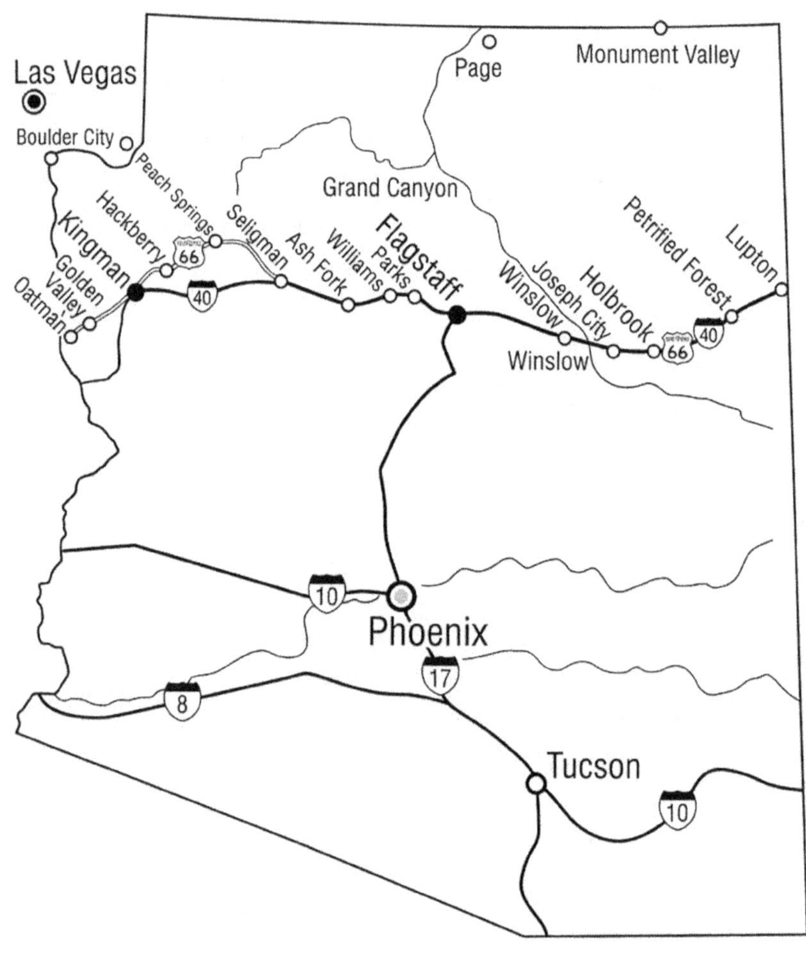

Las Vegas
Boulder City
Peach Springs
Hackberry
Kingman
Golden Valley
Oatman
66
40
Seligman
Ash Fork
Williams
Parks
Flagstaff
Grand Canyon
Page
Monument Valley
Winslow
Joseph City
Holbrook
Winslow
66
40
Petrified Forest
Lupton
10
Phoenix
8
17
Tucson
10
ARIZONA MAP

Chapter 13

ARIZONA

If you thought you'd seen it all, Arizona is here to prove you wrong – with a cheeky grin and a tumbleweed or two. Welcome to the **Grand Canyon State**, where Route 66 stretches out across high deserts, dips through pine forests, and careens over wild mountain passes like it's trying to pack every adventure imaginable into one state. By the time Route 66 gets to Arizona, it's in full-on legend mode. This is the land of **storybook Americana** and natural wonders side by side. One minute you're "standing on a corner in Winslow, Arizona" humming that Eagles tune (you bet we built a park for that, complete with a bronze statue and a red flatbed Ford – we *lean in* to our pop culture moments). The next, you're staring into a gigantic meteor crater in the earth, or wandering among petrified logs older than T-Rex at Petrified Forest National Park. Arizona's portion of the Mother Road has range – in scenery, in stories, and in sheer wow factor.

Start in the east, where 66 rolls in from New Mexico near Holbrook. Right away you know you're in the quirky West: how? **Dinosaurs**. Big pink and green dinos loom over a trading post, advertising petrified wood and kitschy souvenirs. Holbrook itself lets you sleep in a wigwam — the famous Wigwam Motel still offers concrete wigwam rooms that are snug, retro, and unmistakably Route 66. If you feel a childish glee sleeping in a faux-campground circle with classic cars parked out front, blame Arizona. This state specializes in **childlike wonder**. And it's not all make-believe, either. A short detour and you're gazing out over the Painted Desert's rainbow of badlands, or touching 200-million-year-old petrified logs that sparkle with quartz. Even the ground here tells a technicolor story.

Heading on, you'll hit Winslow (snap that photo on *the* corner – you know you want to), then the road aims you toward Flagstaff, a cool mountain town where pines and Route 66 harmonize under clean alpine air. But before that, maybe you veer off to see the **Meteor Crater** – the best-preserved meteor impact site on Earth. Standing on the rim of that colossal hole is humbling; it's like Mother Nature said "surprise!" with a space rock. When you've had your fill of giant craters and galaxies (Flagstaff has an observatory that discovered Pluto, after all), Route 66 says goodbye to the interstate for a while and takes you on the **original two-lane blacktop** through the hearty core of Arizona's 66 culture: Seligman, Peach Springs, Hackberry, Kingman, and Oatman – names that ring like a cowboy ballad.

Seligman is often hailed as the "Birthplace of Historic Route 66," thanks to one Angel Delgadillo, the local barber who in 1987 basically jump-started the preservation movement. Stop in at

Angel & Vilma's gift shop (his old barber shop) and you might meet the nonagenarian Angel himself, still enthusiastically telling travelers to slow down and enjoy life. Seligman revels in pure 1950s kitsch – vintage cars on the street, signs shouting "Route 66" every which way, and the Snow Cap Drive-In slinging ice cream and pranks in equal measure. It's like the town decided the clock stopped in 1960 and nobody told them otherwise. The result? A joyous time warp of Americana.

After Peach Springs, Hackberry, and Kingman, the road gets properly wild, twisting through the Black Mountains on its way to Oatman. Hang on tight and channel your inner road warrior, because the curves to Oatman will test your mettle (and your brakes). What awaits in Oatman is worth every hairpin turn: a living ghost town that refuses to die, mostly because it's having too much fun. Oatman looks straight out of a Western movie set, except it's real – wooden sidewalks, saloons with creaky doors, and yes, those are **burros** walking the streets. Descendants of miners' donkeys, these friendly (and always hungry) burros own the town now. They'll nuzzle up to you looking for carrot snacks; it's like a petting zoo where the animals roam and the tourists are fenced (okay, not literally fenced, but the burros run the show). Stick around for the high-noon shootout (staged drama for laughs) and grab a sarsaparilla at the Oatman Hotel, where Clark Gable honeymooned among the peeling floral wallpaper and thousands of dollar bills tacked to the walls. It's half tourist trap, half legit history, and 100% a blast. You can't make this stuff up – and in Arizona, you don't need to.

By the time you leave Kingman, wind through Oatman, and point yourself toward California, you've crossed **vast deserts,**

high plateaus, and slices of small-town heaven. Arizona's Route 66 experience is an ode to the open road in all its forms. It's the nostalgic neon and Mid-century mojo of places like Kingman (don't miss Mr. D'z diner for a root beer float), and it's the natural splendor of places untouched by time. It's a place where you can drive for miles with nothing but railroad tracks and distant mesas as company, then stumble onto a cozy cafe in a one-horse town serving the best frybread tacos or pecan pie you've ever had. Arizona will let you barrel down an empty stretch at sunset, radio up, wind in your hair, feeling like the hero of some western road film – then it'll throw a curve (literally and figuratively) that forces you to slow down, grin, and say, "Well, *dang* – would you look at that!" From the lone surviving arrow near Winona marking a long-gone trading post, to the hulking concrete **Giganticus Headicus** statue (a lime-green Easter Island head because... why not?) standing vigil in the middle of nowhere, Arizona keeps the surprises coming to the very end.

So go on, ride into our sunset. We promise it'll be a stunner – the kind of deep orange and purple sky that makes you understand why people fall in love with the Southwest. And as you roll on toward that California line, don't be surprised if a part of you wants to turn around and do it all over again. Arizona has that effect. After all, **here** on Route 66, the spirit of the road isn't just alive – it's kicking up dust and daring you to chase it.

Diners, Drive-Ins & Cafés

- **Delgadillo's Snow Cap Drive-In – Seligman, AZ:** The mother of all Route 66 fun stops. Founded in 1953 by prankster Juan Delgadillo, this little drive-in still serves tasty burgers and malts with a side of *silliness* (prepare for goofy signs and joking staff). The roofline is bedecked with old toys and junk, and the "entrance" door handle might be on the wrong side. It's a must-experience slice of pure Americana.

- **Westside Lilo's Café – Seligman, AZ:** Famed for its homemade pie and German twist (the owner is German, so you can get bratwurst alongside meatloaf). Lilo's bright yellow sign and cow-print decor lure you off the road for comfort food done right. Order the peanut butter pie – you won't regret it – and soak in the small-town friendliness.

- **Mr. D'z Route 66 Diner – Kingman, AZ:** A turquoise-and-pink 1950s time warp known for hearty diner fare and homemade root beer. Enjoy a classic hamburger and fries in a vinyl booth under portraits of Elvis and Marilyn. With its vintage Coke machine and neon signs, Mr. D'z is so photogenic it might as well come with its own Instagram filter.

- **Oatman Hotel & Saloon – Oatman, AZ:** Step back into the Wild West at this 1902 saloon where Clark Gable honeymooned. Chili, burgers, and cold sarsaparilla are on the menu, but the real garnish is thousands of dollar bills taped to the walls. Watch out for the resident wild burros peeking in – in Oatman, even the donkeys want a bite of your lunch.

Museums & Historic Sites

* **Arizona Route 66 Museum – Kingman, AZ:** Located in Kingman's old powerhouse, it walks you through dioramas of dust bowl migrants, vintage diners, and neon nights. Upstairs, don't miss the model Studebaker on the *actual* chunk of Route 66 pavement – talk about interactive history!

Vintage Motels & Historic Lodging

* **Wigwam Motel (Village #6) – Holbrook, AZ:** Spend the night in one of Route 66's most iconic motel courtyards, where concrete wigwams come with modern comforts and classic cars often decorate the front row. Cozy, kitschy, and undeniably memorable, it lets you sleep inside one of the Mother Road's signature landmarks.
* **La Posada Hotel – Winslow, AZ:** An exquisite 1930 Fred Harvey railroad hotel that's been lovingly restored. It's like stepping into 1930s Southwest luxury – hand-painted glass windows, Southwestern art, and the sublime Turquoise Room restaurant inside. Many call this the finest hotel on Route 66. Come "stand on the corner" in Winslow, then spend the night in elegance where Hollywood stars once stayed.
* **Hotel Monte Vista – Flagstaff, AZ:** A 1927 downtown hotel steeped in history (and a few ghost stories). Past guests include Elvis and John Wayne. Rooms are vintage chic with views of bustling Flagstaff. Downstairs is a classic cocktail lounge. It's right on the pre-1947 Route 66 alignment, so

you can walk the historic district and then spend the night where legends roamed – maybe even the friendly resident ghosts will say howdy.

Canyon Motel & RV Park – Williams, AZ: Sleep in a caboose! This 1939 motor court in Williams not only offers vintage-style motel rooms but also retired railway cabooses converted into suites. The property backs up to pine forests and even has an underground bomb shelter turned indoor pool. For a gateway to the Grand Canyon (via the train) or Route 66 adventures, this is one unique base camp.

Red Garter Inn B&B – Williams, AZ: How about a night in an 1897 saloon and bordello? This historic B&B on Williams' main strip (an early Route 66 alignment) offers beautifully furnished rooms named after former "ladies" of the establishment. Fresh-baked muffins from the bakery downstairs await in the morning. It's a perfect mix of Wild West lore and Victorian charm – you'll be *resting* in a place where others... um...didn't get much rest.

Aztec Motel & Creative Space – Seligman, AZ: A smartly revived Route 66 stay mixing retro soul with clean, modern comfort. The property feels welcoming rather than precious, and the shared creative space gives it the easygoing energy of a traveler's clubhouse right in the heart of Seligman.

El Trovatore Motel – Kingman, AZ: Known for its long neon sign along the building spelling out "El Trovatore." This 1939 motel has themed rooms (Marilyn Monroe, James Dean) and a gigantic painted map of Route 66 on the hill behind it. Family-run with a personal touch, it's a kitschy delight. At night the neon glows bright red, luring travelers like moths to a very retro flame.

- **Tin Can Alley on 66 – Kingman, AZ:** A cluster of restored vintage Airstreams turned into one of the freshest stays on the Mother Road. It's playful, photogenic, and planted right in downtown Kingman, giving you retro style without pretending the calendar stopped in 1955.

Roadside Attractions & Oddities

- **Chief Yellowhorse Trading Post – Lupton, AZ:** Just inside Arizona at Navajo land, tucked between red cliffs, this historic trading post dates to the 1950s. Huge lettering "HERE IT IS... CHIEF YELLOWHORSE" greets you, along with a giant fiberglass Indian chief and teepee out front. The Yellowhorse family has sold Native crafts here for three generations. Even if you don't shop, stop for the towering rock backdrop and the novelty of a roadside attraction that's part genuine commerce, part vintage roadside showmanship. It's a last (or first) taste of the Southwest's cultural flair on your Route 66 journey.

- **Petrified Forest National Park & Painted Desert – AZ:** Where Mother Nature shows off along Route 66. An original alignment of 66 actually ran through the park – today it's marked by a 1932 Studebaker rusting in the desert. Marvel at the *Painted Desert's* badlands in hues of pink, purple, and gray, then see the *Petrified Forest* – 200-million-year-old logs turned to multicolor stone. There are short trails among the petrified wood; touch these quartz logs and feel the eons. It's a serene, otherworldly landscape that leaves you in awe – and maybe pondering the tiny blip of time that humans have been crossing this terrain.

- **Holbrook Dinosaurs (at Geronimo's Trading Post) – Holbrook, AZ:** Along 66 east of Holbrook lurk dino replicas advertising rock shops. The most famous: a trio of brightly painted concrete dinos at Geronimo's – including a T. rex and brontosaurus that have seen better days but still delight travelers. Pull over to snap a selfie with these Jurassic giants amid the petrified wood stands. They're campy, they're weather-beaten, and they're emblematic of mid-century "roadside zoo" flair. After the Petrified Forest, it's like the dinosaurs came back to life – sort of.

- **Jack Rabbit Trading Post – Joseph City, AZ:** "HERE IT IS" proclaims the famous billboard with a giant jackrabbit silhouette. And here it is indeed – a rustic trading post from 1949 still hopping with souvenirs. Outside, a big fiberglass Jackrabbit invites you to "stand on me" for a photo. Inside, you'll find everything from jackalope magnets to Route 66 snacks. It's touristy, corny, and absolutely essential – after hundreds of miles of "Here It Is" signs, you *have* to stop. And yes, get the T-shirt with that slogan while you're at it.

- **Standin' on the Corner Park – Winslow, AZ:** An intersection turned shrine to the Eagles' song "Take It Easy." There's a life-size bronze of a dude with a guitar, a flatbed Ford truck parked nearby ("it's a girl, my lord..."), and a mural with a girl in a flatbed Ford reflected in a window. Tourists come from everywhere to snap photos "standin' on the corner in Winslow, Arizona" – because how can you not? The song put Winslow on the map, and the town leaned in with this playful, heartfelt park. It's a catchy bit of Americana where music and place entwine – you'll be humming for the next hundred miles.

Meteor Crater – Winslow, AZ: The best-preserved meteorite impact crater on Earth. A short jaunt south of 66, it's nearly a mile across and 550 feet deep – basically a giant hole that screams "Whoa!" Built-up viewing platforms let you peer in, and the visitor center offers cool space rock exhibits. Standing on the rim, you might feel like a tiny astronaut on an alien world. One tip: hold onto your hat; the winds *will* try to launch it into space. It's an out-of-this-world detour that literally hits hard.

Two Guns Ghost Town – Two Guns, AZ: The ruins of a once-thriving 66 tourist stop with a grim history. Two Guns had a zoo, a "Mystery Cave," and a kitschy Old West vibe. Now you'll find crumbling stone buildings, a decaying bridge over Canyon Diablo, and graffiti everywhere. It's eerie and fascinating – infamous for the tale of the Apache Death Cave (a violent legend that gave Two Guns its name). Explore respectfully (watch for snakes and loose bricks) and you'll feel like you've entered a post-apocalyptic movie set. Creepy? A bit. But for adventurous souls, it's a highlight of offbeat Route 66 exploration.

Twin Arrows – near Winona, AZ: One giant red-and-yellow arrow still stands at the old trading-post site, a weathered survivor from one of Route 66's most photogenic ruins. The missing twin somehow makes the place feel even more haunting.

Angel & Vilma's Original Route 66 Gift Shop – Seligman, AZ: The birthplace of Route 66's revival. Angel Delgadillo, the "Guardian Angel of Route 66," started the first historic Route 66 Association here in 1987. His barbershop-turned-gift shop is packed with 66 souvenirs and international license plates covering the walls. If you're lucky, you'll meet Angel himself (in his 90s and still shaving folks) or his family who carry on the legacy. Angel Delgadillo's former barbershop is now a gift shop, museum, and gathering place for road pilgrims. On some days Angel still drops by to greet travelers, while his family carries the story forward with warmth, humor, and deep pride.

Grand Canyon Caverns – Peach Springs, AZ: A 210-foot deep dry cave accessible by elevator, with guided tours that include a room where you can even *spend the night* underground. Outside, there's a giant dinosaur (because why not?) and classic cars. The caverns were once billed as a bomb shelter (they stockpiled supplies in the Cold War). Today, tours show you sparkling limestone formations and one mysterious mummified bobcat. It's a cool, quirky side-stop off 66 – and if you're not up for exploring, at least say hi to the big fake T. rex out front, who's great at photo-bombing.

Hackberry General Store – Hackberry, AZ: A time-warp general store museum on a lonely stretch of 66. Vintage gas pumps, classic Corvettes, rusty signs and old soda machines set the stage outside. Inside, it's jammed with 50s memorabilia and souvenirs – and often a sweet dog roaming around. This place feels like the *heart* of Route 66:

unassuming, authentic, and welcoming. Buy a cold Route 66 Root Beer and chat with whoever's behind the counter. When you leave, you'll swear the sky is a little bluer and the road a little smoother – that's the Hackberry magic.

Giganticus Headicus – Antares, AZ: A 14-foot tall lime-green Easter Island-style head lurking at Antares Point. Built in 2004 by an artist at an otherwise standard-looking gift shop, it's delightfully absurd. Park and gawk at this big green noggin, take a selfie with its blank stare, and ponder the artistic statement (or lack thereof). Some say it's an alien idol, others just a bit of roadside whimsy – either way, it's hard to miss and impossible not to grin at.

Cool Springs Station – Oatman Road, AZ: A restored 1926 stone gas station nestled in the scenic hills before the Oatman pass. Once a lifeline for overheated Model Ts, it's now a mini-museum and gift shop. The surrounding vistas are gorgeous; old foundations and vintage postcards inside tell its tale (it even exploded in a 1960s movie scene!). Buy a cold soda, chat with the proprietor about the treacherous old road, and cool off in the shade of Cool Springs. It's a serene spot that harks back to when gas stations were literally oases in the wild.

Oatman Ghost Town & Wild Burros – Oatman, AZ: A one-of-a-kind former gold mining town clinging to 66's winding alignment through the Black Mountains. Burros (descendants of miners' donkeys) roam the streets begging for carrots. Shops and saloons line the wooden boardwalks. There's daily staged *gunfights* at high noon that delight tourists. It's half tourist trap, half authentic Old West throwback – and wholly entertaining. Be sure to visit the Oatman

Hotel to see Clark Gable's honeymoon suite and thousands of dollar bills taped to the walls. Oatman is that rare place where Route 66 meets the Wild West, and the Wild West wins – truly an **ass**-tonishing stop (sorry, had to).

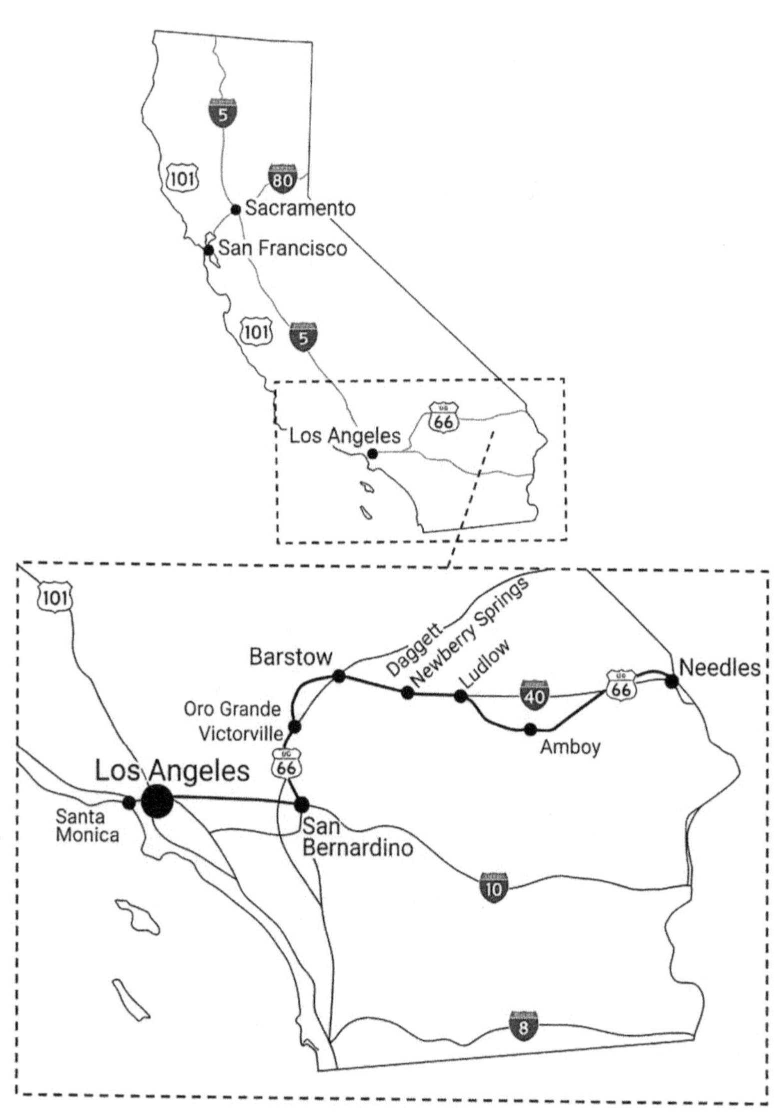

CALIFORNIA MAP

Chapter 14

CALIFORNIA

Finally, California! You've made it to the **final act** of Route 66, and trust us, the Mother Road saved some of its best tricks for last. The Golden State's stretch of 66 is like a three-part epic: it begins with the **Mojave Desert** testing your mettle, transitions into citrus-scented valleys and roadside suburbia, and ends in a blaze of Pacific Ocean glory. California's personality on Route 66 is as colorful and varied as a Hollywood blockbuster – at times laid-back and sun-kissed, at times weird and wild, and ultimately heartwarming and celebratory. This is the *starring role* Route 66 was born to play, and California delivers the finale with style.

Picture this: you cross the Colorado River from Arizona near Topock, and suddenly you're in California — though at first it still feels like the desert is testing whether you've earned the finale. The Mojave will see if you've got the grit for this journey.

Miles of open, arid land with Joshua trees doing yoga poses in the distance, the sun higher and brighter than it's been, and mirages wiggling on the asphalt. Don't worry, we've peppered the desert with **oases of oddity** to keep you entertained. First up, the one and only **Roy's Motel & Café sign** in Amboy – a towering retro beacon that rises out of the empty landscape like a neon mirage, complete with a mid-century motel frozen in time at its base. It's probably one of the most photographed signs on Route 66, and when you stand there, you half expect to see James Dean leaning against a dusty convertible. It's quiet now (Amboy's more or less a ghost town), but that giant boomerang sign still hums with the memory of travelers past. Snap a pic, feel the uncanny "Twilight Zone" vibe, and carry on – you're living history.

Further along, near Newberry Springs, you can still pull over for a dose of cinematic nostalgia at the **Bagdad Cafe**, made famous by the 1987 cult film of the same name. These days the draw is the atmosphere more than the menu — hand-painted signs, movie lore, license plates from around the world, and the distinct feeling that the desert itself decided to open a souvenir stand.

But we're not done with the desert quirk. Ever seen a forest made of bottles? You will – at **Elmer's Bottle Tree Ranch** in Oro Grande, where one man's whimsical vision turned old glass bottles and metal scrap into a sparkling grove of "trees". When the sun hits it, the whole place glitters and chimes; it's oddly peaceful, undeniably strange, and totally California.

As Route 66 enters the greater Los Angeles area, it takes on a new guise: the **dream factory** era of the road. These were the final miles for countless Okies and migrants during the Dust Bowl – the promised land, where palm trees lined the streets and opportunity lurked in every stucco bungalow. Today, you'll thread through cities and towns that grew up with the automobile: San Bernardino, where the last Wigwam Motel offers you one more chance to sleep in a teepee (a neat bookend if you stayed in one back in Holbrook, Arizona); Pasadena, where the Mother Road once ran before being rerouted, home to the marvelous Colorado Street Bridge (an old gem nicknamed "Suicide Bridge" with a gorgeous view and some Hollywood cameos under its belt); and West Hollywood, where a certain greasy spoon named **Barney's Beanery** became rock-star central and cheekily claims to be Route 66's end with a sign inside (don't be fooled, but hey, grab chili and soak up the vibe). By the time you hit Santa Monica Boulevard, you'll feel the Pacific breeze sneaking in. Each mile brings more palm trees, more traffic lights, and perhaps a tinge of bittersweet excitement – the kind you get when a great journey is about to wrap up.

And then California gives you one last Route 66 lesson: the ending moved. Before the road was pushed west, its downtown Los Angeles terminus stood at Broadway and 6th Street. Later, the official western end settled at Lincoln Boulevard and Olympic Boulevard in Santa Monica, where Route 66 met U.S. 101A. It is a plainspoken corner, which somehow feels exactly right. After 2,400 miles, the Mother Road doesn't need fireworks to prove where it ends.

Of course, most travelers still keep rolling to the Santa Monica Pier, and nobody can blame them. The pier is the road's symbolic curtain call — gulls overhead, carnival lights blinking, the Pacific spreading out behind the famous "End of the Trail" sign. So do both if you can: take the official photo at Lincoln and Olympic, then walk the pier for the emotional finale. One gives you the history. The other gives you the feeling.

That may be California's best Route 66 trick of all. The road ends with equal parts fact and myth, asphalt and ocean breeze. Stand at the sign, listen to the surf a few blocks away, and let it sink in: the Mother Road carried you all the way from Chicago to the edge of the Pacific. Now go get that sunset. You've earned it.

Diners, Drive-Ins & Cafés

- **Emma Jean's Holland Burger Café - Victorville, CA:** A classic greasy spoon dating to 1947, housed in a small lime-green building. They're known for the **Holland Burger** (beef patty on French roll with homemade relish) and fresh fruit shakes. As seen on *Diners, Drive-Ins and Dives*, Emma Jean's serves authenticity on a plate - it's the real deal where the locals eat.

- **Fair Oaks Pharmacy & Soda Fountain - South Pasadena, CA:** Actually on the original 1926-30 Route 66 alignment through Pasadena, this 1915 drugstore-turned-soda-fountain is worth a slight detour. Sit on a stool and enjoy an old-fashioned ice cream soda or phosphates amid vintage apothecary decor. It's sugary nostalgia done right – prescription for a sweet time included.

☕ **Barney's Beanery – West Hollywood, CA:** An infamous Route 66-adjacent roadhouse (since 1920) that became a rock 'n' roll hangout. Janis Joplin had her last meal here, and legends from Jim Morrison to Quentin Tarantino frequented it. The chili is legendary, the beer is cold, and the atmosphere is dive-bar meets Hollywood. (Look up and you'll see a sign falsely claiming "Route 66 Ends Here" inside – a cheeky nod to how beloved this joint is by roadtrippers).

Museums & Historic Sites

✳ **Route 66 Mother Road Museum – Barstow, CA:** Tucked in the historic Casa del Desierto Harvey House, it's a treasure trove of Mother Road memorabilia. Vintage postcards, antique gas pumps, and a friendly curator ready with stories – consider it Barstow's scrapbook of Route 66.

✳ **California Route 66 Museum – Victorville, CA:** Fun, funky, and full of photo ops (ever wanted to sit in a neon-lit 1950s VW "photobooth"?). This volunteer-run gem displays everything from Hula Girl lamps to an *Owens Valley* road sign – capturing the highway's spirit in an old roadhouse.

✳ **Original McDonald's Site & Museum – San Bernardino, CA:** On the site of the world's first McDonald's (1948), this unofficial museum is stuffed with retro Golden Arches goodies. From vintage menus to a statues galore, it's a kitschy homage to fast-food history (no fries for sale, but plenty of nostalgia on the menu).

Vintage Motels & Historic Lodging

* **Route 66 Motel – Barstow, CA:** A classic 1920s motel with a fabulous retro sign boasting "Room Phones" and "Color TV" (ooh!). The courtyard features old vintage cars and memorabilia as a free open-air museum for guests. Rooms are basic but clean, and the owner's passion for 66 shines. It's a budget-friendly blast from the past – even the neon cactus on the sign looks like it hasn't aged a day.

* **Wigwam Motel (Village #7) – Rialto/San Bernardino, CA:** "Have You Slept in a Wigwam Lately?" This 1949 motel offers 19 teepee-shaped rooms arranged in a circle. Palm trees sway, a kidney-shaped pool beckons, and at night the wigwams glow with soft light. An unforgettable SoCal rest stop that proves some kitsch is timeless – it's camping *and* glamping rolled into one concrete cone.

* **Aztec Hotel – Monrovia, CA:** A 1925 Mayan Revival marvel that stands out like...well, an Aztec temple along Route 66. Currently closed for renovation, its exaggerated zigzag façade and colorful mosaics are still a photo op from the outside. This quirky National Register landmark has hosted everyone from Hollywood elites to route wanderers – proof that Route 66 isn't just motels and diners, it's also *Art Deco on steroids. (Stay tuned for its hopeful reopening!)*

* **Saga Motor Hotel – Pasadena, CA:** Located on Route 66's former alignment in Pasadena, this 1950s motel is mid-century modest at its best. Famous for its iconic neon **saga** horse sign and a heated pool that's seen countless cannonballs, the Saga offers old-fashioned hospitality. It's walking

distance to vintage diners and shops on Colorado Blvd. – a perfect last stop before the final run to Santa Monica.

Roadside Attractions & Oddities

- **Road Runner's Retreat – near Chambless, CA:** About 10 miles east of Amboy, this long-shuttered desert stop still rises out of the Mojave with one of California's great Route 66 signs — a giant roadrunner neon landmark first raised in the 1960s and brought back to life in 2025 after decades of darkness. The café was lost to fire in 2020, but the mural survived, and the restored sign now makes this one of the Mojave's most stirring comeback stories.

- **Roy's Motel & Café Neon Sign – Amboy, CA:** The iconic mid-century **Roy's** boomerang neon sign still rises tall against the Mojave sky. Though Amboy is nearly deserted, the gas station and café have reopened (limited hours). It feels like a Twilight Zone set – empty cabins, the deadpan ticking of the Roy's sign if you listen closely. By day, the sign's turquoise and red paint pops; by night, when its neon occasionally flickers to life, it's pure magic. Standing under Roy's sign, you can almost hear the ghosts of travelers past whispering about chicken-fried steak and malts. A must-stop for any Route 66 pilgrim in the California desert.

- **Amboy Crater – Amboy, CA:** A 6,000-year-old volcanic cinder cone rising black and brooding from the flat desert. There's a trail to the top if you're up for a 3-mile hike (best in cooler months). Even from the trailhead, the view is otherworldly. Climb the rim and peer into the crater's bowl – suddenly you feel like you're on Mars. The quiet out here is profound. Amboy Crater proves Route 66 isn't all man-made attractions; nature sometimes steals the show with a literal *bang*.

- **Calico Ghost Town – Yermo, CA:** An old silver mining town turned county park/tourist attraction. Technically a few miles off Route 66, but often visited as a side trip. Stroll the boardwalks, pan for gold, ride the little train. Yes, it's commercialized and a bit campy, but it keeps the spirit of the Old West alive. The hills are dotted with mine shafts and the buildings (some original, some reconstructed) house museums and shops. Consider it a chance to stretch your legs and play cowboy before rejoining the modern freeway. Bonus: great photo ops, especially the giant "Calico" sign on the mountain like a wild west Hollywood.

- **Casa del Desierto (Harvey House) – Barstow, CA:** A stunning 1911 railroad depot and Harvey House hotel, beautifully restored, now housing museums and an events center. Its grand arches and tan brick façade rise unexpectedly from the desert – a true mirage of elegance for early travelers. Even if the museums are closed, walk around back: twin staircases and a courtyard evoke the days when well-heeled rail passengers dined here in style. It's a striking contrast to the dusty town of Barstow – a *desert castle* that stands as a monument to the hospitality of yesteryear.

- **Elmer's Bottle Tree Ranch – Oro Grande, CA:** A forest of "bottle trees" – metal rods welded into trunk and branch shapes, adorned with over 200 colorful glass bottles that clink in the breeze. Created by the late Elmer Long, this whimsical art environment invites wandering. You'll discover all sorts of found-object treasures hanging among the bottles: typewriters, wagon wheels, even a *Noddy* car. When the sun hits the glass, it's a kaleidoscope. It's peaceful, bizarre, and oddly moving. If you can, go at sunset when the light makes the bottles glow – it's pure Route 66 magic, turning junk into a jewel.

Cucamonga Service Station – Rancho Cucamonga, CA: A beautifully restored 1915 gas station with a mission-style flair, now a small museum. It has vintage gravity pumps out front and period-correct signage. This station is a rare survivor from the **birth of the highway** era – predating even Route 66. It won awards for the restoration and once you see it, you'll know why. It's cute as a button and exudes early-20th-century charm. Stop for a quick photo and maybe honk to thank the local historic society folks if they're around.

Colorado Street Bridge – Pasadena, CA: A majestic 1913 concrete arch bridge that carried early Route 66 traffic into Pasadena. Nicknamed "Suicide Bridge" for the unfortunate souls who leapt from it during the Great Depression, it's also famous from movies and legend. Today it's a pedestrian vista point (and still carries cars) offering sweeping views of the Arroyo Seco. The ornate lamp posts and elegant curves make it one of the most beautiful bridges in America. Walk it at dusk if you can – it's eerily romantic. Just don't think about the ghosts... focus on that California sunset instead.

Santa Monica Terminus & Pier – Santa Monica, CA: For the official finish, head to Lincoln Boulevard and Olympic Boulevard, where Route 66 historically ended after its westward extension. Then keep rolling to the Santa Monica Pier for the emotional encore — the famous "End of the

Trail" sign, carnival lights, gulls, and Pacific breeze. One stop gives you the history. The other gives you the postcard.

For one last badge of honor, swing by the 66-to-Cali booth on the pier, where travelers can pick up a Route 66 completion certificate to prove they made it all the way to the Pacific.

The Best Darn Bait
But we do Supply
With a Date
Provide you
We Can't
Burma-Shave
U.S. 66
The Mother Road

Chapter 15

ROUTE 66 HALL OF FAME

Top Rated Diner

Lou Mitchell's (Chicago, IL) – A legendary start-of-the-road eatery, open since 1923 and famous for its hearty breakfasts and hospitality. Located just a mile from Route 66's starting point, it greets travelers with free donut holes while they wait and fluffy omelets that earn rave reviews. Lou Mitchell's enduring charm and tradition (they even hand out Milk Duds to newcomers) make it arguably the most beloved diner on the Mother Road.

Honorable Mention: *The Ariston Café* (Litchfield, IL) – Opened in 1924 (before Route 66 existed), this family-run restaurant is one of the oldest on 66 and is on the National Register of Historic Places. Renowned for its warm service and diverse menu, the Ariston has been a Mother Road favorite for generations.

Top Rated Hotel

Blue Swallow Motel (Tucumcari, NM) – A meticulously preserved 1939 motor court that tops many Route 66 travelers' lists. The Blue Swallow's vintage rooms (many with adjoining garages) and glowing neon sign offer an authentic step back in time. It's *"one of the most celebrated motels on Route 66,"* still operating in its original layout and delighting guests with retro charm and hospitality.

Honorable Mention: *Wigwam Motel* (Holbrook, AZ) – Sleep in a concrete teepee at this kitschy 1950s icon. One of only two surviving Wigwam Villages on Route 66, it's so storied that Pixar's **Cars** immortalized it as the Cozy Cone Motel in Radiator Springs. Staying here – with classic cars often parked by each wigwam – is a bucket-list novelty for Mother Road enthusiasts.

Top Rated Attraction

Cadillac Ranch (Amarillo, TX) – This striking roadside art installation features ten classic Cadillacs buried nose-first in a Texas field. It's a *"quintessential Route 66 experience,"* inviting visitors to bring spray paint and add their own colorful graffiti to the constantly evolving cars. Cadillac Ranch's blend of interactive art and pop culture vibe has made it one of the highway's most popular and photographed stops.

Honorable Mention: *Petrified Forest National Park* (Arizona) – The only national park traversed by Route 66, showcasing otherworldly Painted Desert vistas and 225-million-year-old petrified wood. A portion of old Route 66 runs through the park, marked by a 1932 Studebaker relic – a silent reminder of Mother Road travelers past. The Petrified Forest brilliantly combines natural wonder with Route 66 history in one stop.

Most Photographed Place

Santa Monica Pier – "End of the Trail" Sign (Santa Monica, CA) – The pier is Route 66's most photographed symbolic finish, even though the official western terminus is inland at Lincoln and Olympic. With the sign, Ferris wheel, and Pacific Ocean all in one frame, it remains the ultimate celebratory photo op for Mother Road travelers.

Honorable Mention: *Blue Whale of Catoosa* (Catoosa, OK) – A goofy 20-foot blue whale statue beside a pond, originally built in 1972 as an anniversary gift. This grinning whale has become one of Route 66's most photogenic roadside attractions, delighting travelers of all ages. It's *"one of Route 66's most photographed attractions,"* beckoning road-trippers to snap a souvenir photo inside its smiling mouth.

Most Famous Neon Sign

Roy's Motel & Café (Amboy, CA) – The towering neon sign at this isolated desert outpost is pure Americana and arguably the Mother Road's most iconic sign. Erected in the 1950s in stylized Googie splendor, the **ROY'S** sign stands 50 feet tall and was restored to glowing form in 2019. It's the tallest thing for miles in the Mojave and even *"claims to be the most photographed on Route 66"*. When lit at night, Roy's neon beckons travelers through the darkness – a radiant symbol of Route 66's mid-century glory.

Honorable Mention: *Munger Moss Motel* (Lebanon, MO) – This classic 1940s motor court boasts a gorgeous vintage neon sign that was lovingly restored in 2010. Its red-and-blue **Munger Moss** script and arrow have welcomed Route 66 travelers for decades. A *"shining example of the retro neon signage that Route 66 is famous for,"* the Munger Moss sign still lights up the Missouri night as a living piece of Mother Road nostalgia.

Most Featured Section in Cinema

Flagstaff, Arizona & Environs – Northern Arizona's stretch of Route 66 has starred in numerous films. Downtown Flagstaff and nearby highways appear in iconic road movies like *Easy Rider* (1969) and *National Lampoon's Vacation* (1983), as well as the indie hit *Little Miss Sunshine* (2006). With its classic small-town strip and scenic desert vistas, the Flagstaff area has been a go-to location for capturing Route 66's historic atmosphere on film. Time and again, Hollywood cameras have rolled on this portion of the Mother Road, making it arguably the route's most cinematically famous section.

Honorable Mention: *Amboy, California* – The tiny ghost town of Amboy (and its landmark Roy's Café) has an almost otherworldly look that filmmakers love. This lonely desert locale on old Route 66 has been used as a backdrop for several productions, especially thrillers and horror films. For example, the mystery film *Beneath the Dark* (2010) was set largely at Roy's Motel, taking full advantage of Amboy's eerie, time-capsule ambiance. If a movie scene calls for a "middle-of-nowhere" Route 66 vibe, Amboy often gets the call.

Best Individual Food Item

The 72-Ounce Steak Challenge – Big Texan Steak Ranch (Amarillo, TX) – No food on Route 66 is more notorious than this giant steak dinner. The Big Texan's *free-if-you-finish* 72 oz. steak (with all the trimmings) in under an hour has been a carnivorous rite of passage since the 1960s. Served in a lively cowboy-themed roadhouse, the massive steak is less about gourmet finesse than about bragging rights and bucket-list legend. Whether you attempt the challenge or just watch others try, the experience at the Big Texan is an unforgettable (and uniquely Route 66) spectacle.

Honorable Mention: *Ted Drewes "Concrete" Frozen Custard* (St. Louis, MO) – A sweet Mother Road tradition. Ted Drewes has been serving creamy frozen custard on Route 66 since the 1930s, and in 1959 it invented the **"concrete"** – a malt so thick it's handed to you upside-down. This ultra-rich custard, blended with mix-ins, has achieved legendary status. On any summer night, you'll find lines of travelers and locals at the Chippewa Street stand, all craving a taste of this **95-year-old Route 66 icon** that absolutely lives up to the hype.

Best Route 66 Museum

Illinois Route 66 Hall of Fame & Museum (Pontiac, IL) – A top-notch museum dedicated to the history and memorabilia of the Mother Road. Housed in a historic firehouse, it's packed with nostalgic exhibits about classic Route 66 businesses and personalities. The museum's crown jewels are the vehicles of legendary Route 66 artist and "road warrior" Bob Waldmire – his VW hippie van and his famed converted school bus home ("Road Yacht") are on display here. Visitors can literally walk through Waldmire's bus and see his quirky personal touches, making this museum a pilgrimage site for 66 enthusiasts. From highway signs and diner booths to folk art and photographs, Pontiac's collection beautifully **celebrates the spirit and stories of Route 66** for all who can't get enough of the Mother Road.

Can't Get Enough of Route 66?

If you're craving more Mother Road magic, Hollywood and television have plenty to offer. Over the years Route 66 has played a meaningful role in numerous films and TV shows – sometimes as a central character, other times as an unforgettable backdrop. Here are some of the most notable:

The Grapes of Wrath (1940) – John Steinbeck's classic Dust Bowl saga follows the Joad family's hard journey from Oklahoma to California **along Route 66**, capturing the highway's importance as the "road of flight" during the Great Depression. This Oscar-winning film introduced the world to the idea of Route 66 as the *"Mother Road"* (a term Steinbeck coined in the novel) and cemented its place in American cultural history.

"Route 66" *(1960–1964, TV series)* – The show that put Route 66 into every living room. This weekly CBS drama followed two friends (played by Martin Milner and George Maharis) cruising America in a Chevy Corvette and looking for adventure. Uniquely, the series was filmed **on location in towns across Route 66 and beyond**, so episodes took place in dozens of different communities. With its on-the-road storytelling, *Route 66* the TV show showcased the diversity of the highway and inspired many road-trip dreams.

Easy Rider *(1969)* – The seminal counterculture road movie starring Peter Fonda and Dennis Hopper. *Easy Rider* follows two biker-hippies riding west to New Orleans, and parts of their trip were filmed *along Route 66* (notably in Flagstaff, Arizona). The film's imagery of endless highway and open freedom – set to a rock soundtrack – helped mythologize Route 66 during a time when the road itself was fading from prominence.

Bagdad Cafe *(1987)* – A quirky indie gem set at a rundown truck-stop cafe and motel on a remote stretch of Route 66 in the Mojave Desert. Although named after the town of Bagdad, CA (a now-abandoned Route 66 site), it was **filmed at the then-called Sidewinder Cafe in Newberry Springs, CA** – which has since been renamed "Bagdad Café" in honor of the movie. The film's offbeat story and the lonely desert setting struck a chord, turning the real Bagdad Cafe into a minor pilgrimage site for film buffs traveling 66.

Cars *(2006)* – Pixar's animated love letter to Route 66. (See the dedicated section above for more detail.) In short, *Cars* brought Route 66's spirit to a worldwide audience of kids and adults, with its tale of a forgotten small town and the glory days of cruising the two-lane blacktop. Many **real Mother Road landmarks** – from the Cadillac Ranch to cozy motels – are referenced or subtly depicted in the film, making it a treasure hunt of Route 66 easter eggs for fans.

Rain Man *(1988)* – This Oscar-winning drama isn't about Route 66, but it features a **pivotal scene at a Route 66 motel**. When Charlie (Tom Cruise) realizes his brother Raymond (Dustin Hoffman) was the childhood "Rain Man," it happens at the Big 8 Motel in El Reno, Oklahoma – a classic Route 66 motor inn standing in for Amarillo, TX in the film. That emotional scene – with the neon motel sign glowing outside – gave 66 a brief but memorable cameo in a beloved film.

Little Miss Sunshine *(2006)* – A dark comedy about a dysfunctional family road-tripping from New Mexico to California in a VW bus. Several **scenes were filmed on Route 66**, including in downtown Flagstaff, AZ (where the family's van breaks down). The Mother Road setting provides an authentic Americana backdrop as this oddball family chugs westward, underscoring the film's themes of journey and perseverance.

National Lampoon's Vacation *(1983)* – Chevy Chase's Clark Griswold leads his family on a cross-country misadventure from Chicago to L.A., following much of the old Route 66 corridor. The movie features stops in Arizona along 66 – for example, the Griswolds' metallic pea-green Wagon Queen Family Truckster is seen cruising through downtown Flagstaff and they visit a roadside Indian trading post (and even the Grand Canyon). *Vacation*'s mix of roadside attractions and gallows humor made it a road-trip classic – and gave a comic nod to the Mother Road en route.

No Country for Old Men (2007) – In this modern thriller, Route 66 subtly sneaks into the climax. The final motel showdown, set in "El Paso," was actually **filmed on Central Avenue (old Route 66) in Albuquerque, NM**, at the Desert Sands Motel. The film doesn't call attention to it, but sharp-eyed Route 66 fans recognize the vintage motel and neon sign. It's a brief return to the screen for 66, serving as an atmospheric backdrop in a Best Picture-winning film.

Other notable mentions: Numerous other productions have utilized Route 66 locales in passing. The comedy *Wild Hogs* (2007) shot biker bar scenes on Central Avenue in Albuquerque – and reportedly spurred an uptick of motorcycle tourism through New Mexico afterward. Oliver Stone's edgy *Natural Born Killers* (1994) features several sequences on old 66 as its outlaw couple rampage across the Southwest (with filming in Illinois, New Mexico, and Arizona). Even Francis Ford Coppola's *The Outsiders* (1983) was filmed in Tulsa along Route 66's path, using the road's mid-20th-century neighborhoods to evoke the early 1960s setting. And of course, countless documentaries and travelogues (from Billy Connolly's travel series to **Michael Wallis's** PBS specials) have paid homage to the Mother Road on screen.

Whether it's through classic dramas, quirky comedies, or animated adventures, Route 66's presence in film and TV has helped immortalize the allure of America's most famous highway. These on-screen portrayals let us revisit the romance, struggles, and fun of Route 66 anytime – and they often inspire viewers to get out there and experience "The Main Street of America" for themselves.

For additional copies,
Support your local Route 66 restop
or visit us at Lifeimpactpublishing.com.